THE BIBLE AS BEDTIME STORY

And Other Essays on Religion & Culture

BRIAN G. MATTSON

SWINGING BRIDGE PRESS

For P. Andrew Sandlin,
for your friendship and encouragement.

CONTENTS

FOREWORD BY P. ANDREW SANDLIN

This is a book of systematic theology. The fact that it reads unlike any to which you've been accustomed doesn't mean it's any less a systematic theology. For centuries systematic theology was, with rare exception, written according to academic standards. Systematics was a school textbook, even if written in and for the church. Theology was seen as a science. Its texts read like science texts but with God's revelation as the subject matter. This theology was the chief example of what has been derided as "scholasticism." If you've read Thomas Aquinas or Francis Turretin or Charles Hodge or Wayne Grudem, you know what I'm talking about. Liberals adopted the same format; their conclusions differed from that of conservatives, but their form didn't. Systematic theology was academic, scientific.

Hans Frei's *The Eclipse of Biblical Narrative* (1974) made it safe for theologians to return to a prominent form of theology we find in the Bible: narrative. The Bible is filled with stories, in fact, is one Big Story of God's spectacular creation spoiled by man's sin but being remade by God in his Son Jesus Christ's once-for-all atoning work on the cross and his victorious resurrection and present heavenly rule. Theology written in this story format is closer to the way the Bible conveys truth. Ironically, while theology as narrative seems innovative, it's actually a return to a very old way of writing theology: the old, Bible way.

This book does that. Brian Mattson is an accomplished musician, and he brings his evident artistic gifts to his theologizing. He sees theology as an art as much as a science. He's a theological storyteller. He sacrifices neither art to theology nor theology to art. His theology is a work of beauty as much as a work of truth. Beautiful truth. This book addresses topics as diverse as covenant children, secularism, the Emergent Movement, lessons about God from chess, child-defending fatherhood, postmodern theology, the textual transmission of the Bible, Tiger Woods' worship problem, natural law, same-sex "marriage," Jane Austen, and much more. Like all good systematic theologies, it overturns a lot of cultural stones.

After you read this book (and you can read the chapters in about any order—as long as you read the first chapter first), you'll know a lot more theology. Which means you'll know a lot more about God. And you'll know his revelation not in a systematic, scientific, academic form, but in artistic beauty.

Ours is a beautiful God. His revelation deserves beautiful theologizing. Enter, Brian Mattson.

—*P. Andrew Sandlin*
   President & Founder, *Center For Cultural Leadership*

PREFACE

I have always loved collections of essays. Some of my favorites are volumes by opinion columnists who gather together a "best of" collection from the previous decade. This is a way of resurrecting long-forgotten essays. After all, columns are published in newspapers, something most people discard immediately after reading.

The Internet has solved storage and retrieval problems, but not the problem of forgetting. The only way someone might find an essay of mine from years ago is to already be aware of it, recall it, and to search online specifically by its title. But, as a general rule, most of my writings sit expectantly in a dark, lonely server room in midtown Manhattan, just as forgotten as recycled newsprint.

Perusing through those archives recently, it therefore occurred to me that in this respect there is little difference between the newspaper columnist and the "blogger." Why not publish a "best of" collection of my own? This is the volume you hold in your hands.

Most of the essays were originally published on my website, but not all. The titular essay, "The Bible as Bedtime Story" has never appeared online or in print, nor have two of the longest essays: Chapter 5, "A Very Old Kind of Heresy," and Chapter 38, "On Grace

& Leisure." The entire collection is eclectic and defies sharp organization, so I have decided on two parts: first, my more theologically oriented writings, followed by the more culturally inclined. The very best thing about "collected essays" is that one can open the book at random and enjoy one chapter at a time in no particular order.

I have modestly edited most of these writings and have provided short introductory remarks where context is needed. It is a delight to shine the light of day on these once-lonely texts, and I hope the reader will enjoy them.

❧ I ❧
RELIGION

THE BIBLE AS BEDTIME STORY

O nce upon a time there was a Great King of a realm, and a Usurper arose to make war against him. Recruiting a traitor in high places, his initial attack was a resounding success. The Great King was driven out of his capital city, out of his land, and his own people turned against him. The Usurper took up residence in the King's palace, and placed his followers in the halls of power.

∿

THE GREAT KING remains a very powerful King. Still at his disposal are legions of missiles filled with nuclear warheads, against which the Usurper is utterly powerless. Victory could be instantly his by simply destroying everything, ridding himself forever of this menace. Effective for that purpose, yes, but not if he had other plans in mind. A nuclear holocaust would render his capital city and entire realm useless. He himself might take up residence at some point, but there would be no people, no community, no society to rule. This is *his* city, his realm, and his people. He fashioned it. He loves it. He still has purposes for it. Any claim the Usurper has to his city and his realm is a false claim.

So he waits.

~

TIME PASSES, and sages seek to interpret the Great King's restraint. Why does he allow life to continue under the dominion of the Usurper? Whole schools of philosophy arise with differing interpretations of the Great King's aims. Some say he restrains himself simply because he has loved ones in the city and wants to rescue them out of it. He is planning a rescue operation for those few, they think, and only after will he let the nuclear warheads fall.

Others grant that this would be one way of going about things, but they object, uneasily, that this still grants the Usurper a great and terrible victory. The Great King can only defeat him by destroying his very own kingdom?

Still others think that the Great King might be restraining himself not only because he has loved ones behind enemy lines, but because he is filled with some nostalgia for the place. He knows and remembers the beautiful architecture, the city planning, the way everything is organically laid out, its unity and diversity. It all reflects his own personal style. He remembers the gardens, the woodlands, and the beauty of the seasons. He is reluctant to engage the nuclear warheads. He is giving the city a bit more time to enjoy the wonderful things the realm offers, but he knows that this is merely delaying the inevitable. It will, eventually, have to be destroyed.

A final group is persuaded that the Great King's restraint indicates that he doesn't plan to destroy the realm at all. Perhaps he loves his kingdom, his realm, and his city. Maybe he had grand plans for it that got aborted when he was attacked. Why shouldn't his aim be liberation instead of destruction? These wise men think that the Great King has an old-fashioned infiltration and assault in mind rather than instantaneous destruction. He is gathering strength, allies, and intelligence, and establishing a beachhead, a foothold in preparation for an ultimate D-Day in the fullness of time.

~

SO LIFE GOES on in the realm. The Great King does begin implementing a long term plan. He first establishes a forward outpost, recruiting a single family still living in the realm, winning them back to his side. He clears out a patch of ground where they can live in loyalty to him. This family and this spot of ground are special; unlike the commoners surrounding them, they owe special loyalty to him. There is a great distinction between the special and the common, between them and the rest of the realm. Nevertheless, he lets them in on a secret: this is not the end-game, but a means to an end. This spot of ground where the King's flag is unfurled is a down-payment, a picture of what all will someday be; this patch of ground is, in fact, the entire realm held in trust. The real end-game is for all of the King's people to inherit the whole realm, not just this patch of ground. The Great King's favor to this family, the establishment of this outpost, is part of a far grander plan: stemming from this one family *every other family of the realm* would ultimately be blessed. It is through this outpost, this beachhead, that their redemption will come.

This family greatly expands. It becomes a mini-nation living in the midst of the realm. The Usurper tries time and again to get these meddlesome agitators back to his side. He plies them with false promises in exchange for allegiance, and, like he did with their distant father, that original traitor, has a great deal of success. He is a persuasive adversary.

The Great King sends persuasive emissaries of his own to the people, reminding them of their grand purpose in the world. Those of the outpost were prone to forget that they are an outpost. They were forgetting that the King has designs not just for them, but for the whole realm. They were forgetting that the patch of ground was the beginning, not the end.

From time to time the Great King disciplines and prunes his small outpost. He wants only the faithful involved in this crucial underground movement. He even allows them to be arrested and locked up for a period of time: a wake-up call for the faithful. He wishes to fashion a true resistance movement, those in tune with the strategic plans, for that is the only way D-Day will succeed. So the Great King's outpost narrows over time. Like the armies of Gideon, the nation is whittled down to a faithful few because that is just how the Great King likes it. He likes his victories to come in the form of weakness, not strength.

THE TIME DRAWS NEAR. Its fullness has almost arrived. The Great King sends a Royal Herald to the outpost, declaring that the kingdom is at hand, and commanding all to turn their loyalties back to the Great King. Like General Maximus and the Roman army of old waiting on the Germanic borderlands, they wait in breathless anticipation. They hear hoofbeats. A horse lopes into view, ridden by a headless man. The herald is decapitated. Maximus of old said, "Their answer is no. On my word, unleash hell." The Great King's reply is similar, only he finishes with, "On my word, unleash heaven."

A man arrives in the outpost. Crossing over the river at the borderlands, he speaks his first public words: "The time has come." Weightier words were never heard. "The kingdom is near," he added, "Repent and believe the good news!" D-Day has arrived. This one is the Champion of the Great King, who comes calling all to change their loyalties and pledge allegiance to him. Immediately he unleashes heaven, cleansing the realm. Everywhere he goes, he casts out the Usurper's minions; he heals sickness; he raises the dead. He tells them that if he does these things, then they should know "that the kingdom has come upon them." With the coming of the Champion, the Great King himself has made his entry into the realm, and the demons shudder.

Ultimately, in a bold act of self-sacrifice the Champion lays down his life at the hands of the Usurper, only to take it up again in glorious power. He breaks the ultimate stranglehold the Usurper has over the whole realm: the power of death. The Great King and his Champion wins the decisive victory.

The trumpets blast, the message proclaimed. He rallies all people, not just those living in his original, crucial, little outpost, but people over the whole realm to turn to him in allegiance and to bow their knee to his Majesty. For the outpost resistance movement had achieved its purpose as a beachhead, a landing place for the Champion; now the special relationship overflows its banks and floods the realm, available to all. The Great King makes people in every reach of the realm new and transformed by the power of the Champion's indestructible life. The great liberation has begun.

~

THE KINGDOM HAS ARRIVED. The news is heralded everywhere. The good news of liberation and freedom is for everybody, men, women, and children. What once was curse is now reversed. Darkness is flooded with light, hatred replaced by love, enmity with communion. Oh, there remains resistance. The ultimate power of the Usurper has been destroyed, but he remains a deceiver yet. The Great King now waits for his foe's final destruction. But between this principal victory and ultimate end, he empowers the good news of victory to reverberate throughout the realm. His provision of returning amnesty for repentance converts even the most hardened of old enemies to new friends.

All over the realm, wherever citizens believe the news of victory, things begin to look, feel, sound, and smell very different. There is new ownership; the old, traitorous flag of the Usurper is torn down, as are his monuments and statues, replaced by the standard of a new Sovereign Majesty, one with authority over the totality of heaven and earth.

Life in the realm can never be the same. Colors take on a

different hue, for the blind now see. Sounds are heard as never before, for the deaf now hear. Goods once enjoyed in slavery are now graces enjoyed in freedom. Where once was darkness, there is light. What once was dirty is now clean. What once was sinful, twisted, and disfigured is now just, righted, and restored.

The realm is not even like it was before the Great War. That was a time of pure innocence. This is the time of having-been-liberated: scars and rubble remain for now. Many walk with a limp. This is a far deeper, more mature reality than mere innocence. No, for those liberated by the Great King, there is no sense in which life just goes on as it always has. In nothing is life the same as it has always been. There is no such thing as a "common" life for such as these. The lowly washerwoman no longer hangs the clothes out of mere duty, but with joy and gratitude. The lawyer, liberated from the Father of Lies, advocates and advises with integrity. The painter sees the realm with new eyes and paints it as it really is: the Great King's Dominion. Every common vocation, every nook and cranny of the realm has been changed by the victory of the Great King. And his followers, their hearts changed in allegiance, work to spread the light of the kingdom everywhere there is remaining darkness. What is common is made special because they do all things, eating, drinking, and whatever they do, for the glory, honor, and tribute of their Savior King. They shine like stars in the remaining darkness.

~

ONE DAY the Great King and his Champion will return to finish off the Usurper once and for all, to heal all wounds and scars, wipe away all tears, and to take up his final residence and usher his people into a final great rest. The realm itself will be transformed into a glory it had never known since its founding. It will be cleansed and renovated to the original destiny the Great King had always planned for it. The greatness and totality of his victory is displayed in this: in destroying the Usurper, he did not destroy his own realm.

Far from being annihilated, on that day the whole realm will be sacred and special; everything from the bells on the horses to the pots in the kitchen will be inscribed with the words: "Holy To The Great King."

And they will live happily ever after.

COVENANT BENEFITS

I have just returned from a funeral in Casper, Wyoming.

There were several highlights, and I'd like to share just one. It is one most meaningful to me as a father.

Is there any real benefit to growing up in a Christian home? I know that in the never-ending debate between paedo (infant) and credo-baptists (adult believers only) the "credos" usually assume that there isn't. After all, "all have sinned and fall short of the glory of God." What difference does it really make whether a child, born in sin, comes into the world in a Christian or non-Christian home? Both are in need of salvation, which is brought about by the Holy Spirit. About that both paedo and credo-baptists are agreed.

But the paedo (infant) baptist goes further, believing that the covenant, which always runs through families in the Bible, provides real (though not in and of itself decisive) benefit, real means of grace, to children of believers. History matters. Context matters. Creation itself, with its wide range of relationships, really matters. The ultimate truth that individuals stand before God, either in Christ or outside of him, does not erase or negate earthly realities and proximate truths like one's familial relationships. After all, God created the world of context and relationships. He works in and through them. Being a child of the covenant, being taught that God is *our* God, not just the parents' God until such time as the child makes a "decision," provides very real benefit. The benefit is the covenant itself, the belief and consciousness that Jesus is mine and that God is my father, and that the Holy Spirit effectively communicates Christ to me. Growing up with that kind of consciousness makes a big difference, indeed.

LET ME BACK UP. Years ago, while we were away from our home church in Billings, Montana, our pastor apparently preached a sermon in which he explained what a "benediction" is: a "good word" from God. When a worship service ends, God gets the last word, and it is a word of blessing. Our pastor taught the congregation that they should not bow their heads during a benediction, for it is not a prayer. It is not us talking to God. It is God talking to us. Further, he told them they should receive this blessing from God in their physical actions. They should look up as the pastor delivers the benediction, and they should hold out their hands in front of them, physically "receiving," as it were, this blessing.

When we returned home, this practice was widely in full swing. People held their hands out and looked up to receive the benediction. I never quite got comfortable with it, being a native Presbyterian, and we never use our bodies in worship, much to our shame. But my kids seem to have no such DNA problems.

You should also know, by way of background, that I never have the privilege of receiving the benediction while standing with my children. As a participant in the music ministry, I am always up front when it happens.

VERY FEW PEOPLE at this funeral were Christians. The end of the service came, and the pastor said, "Let us close with a benediction."

To my mild surprise, instinctively, without missing a beat, there was my eldest daughter, ten years old, standing next to me with her hands outstretched. Nobody else in the place did such a thing. A moment passed and she became a bit self-conscious of the fact that she was the only one holding out her hands to receive God's blessing. Slowly but surely, she began to draw her hands back, and I saw it happening.

I reached down and grabbed her hands. I forcefully thrust them out further.

I was not just teaching her a lesson. I was teaching myself a lesson I've been long overdue in learning.

Never, ever, ever let the apathy or ignorance of others around you keep you from receiving the blessing of God. My daughter just knew, without having to wonder or think about it, that this was a word from *her* God, a word of blessing for *her*, and there she was, ready, eager, and willing to receive it. Until the thorns (in this case, a gathering of tares among the wheat) started to choke it out and fill her mind with some doubt about that fact. No! I hated seeing that doubt creep in, and instinctively did what I could to stop it.

It is one thing to grow up wondering if God has a blessing for me. It is quite another to grow up knowing that God has a blessing for me.

Does it make a difference for a ten year old?

I don't think there is any question about it. And the scene of my daughter expectantly standing there with her outstretched hands is a highlight I will treasure deep in my heart.

Treasure, and learn from. My stoic, Presbyterian DNA be damned. This Sunday, I know what my hands will be doing: following my daughter's example.

What do you know? Covenant families do make a difference. And not just for the kids.

❧ 3 ❧
CHRISTIANITY AS A FOREIGN TONGUE

First *Things* published online an article of mine on the collapsing "secular cage" in which the public square has been imprisoned these long hundreds of years.

I do not plan on reading through the comments section over there, as that is rarely useful, and more commonly harmful to my health. I did notice the first few, however. And somebody immediately jumped, on cue, to the predictable response that I was overly "bold" in suggesting that Christianity has anything *unique* to offer of which any number of other religious worldviews couldn't equally boast. His example was Hinduism which, surely, he suggests, also teaches that you shouldn't steal. See? Hindus believe in private property! What could Mattson possibly mean by suggesting that Judeo-Christianity is unique in teaching private property?

Well, let me just say that when Dutch and British colonists arrived in India, they didn't find a bustling and prosperous commercial empire. India did not have a formal *system* of legal private property, and thus lacked the ability to leverage dead capital for economic investment. You can read all about why free enterprise has worked in the West and failed everywhere else in Hernando De Soto's aptly titled, *The Mystery of Capital: Why Capitalism Triumphs in the West and Fails Everywhere Else* (Basic Books, 2003). Anyone who wants to suggest that the Judeo-Christian heritage is irrelevant to the rise and maintenance of Western values faces the inescapable fact that those values have *only* arisen in the Judeo-Christian West.

But this all got me to thinking. It reminded me that one of the knee-jerk reactions to robust Christian advocacy in public is to deny that Christianity has anything unique to offer. Anything good in it, it is supposed, can be found elsewhere and there is therefore no need for it. But this simply isn't true, and it struck home to me just last night.

~

I TOOK my girls to the movie theater. This is such an uncommon occurrence in our household that my daughters, 5 and 9, did not realize that we were actually going to see a movie until we had actually stood in line, purchased tickets, and were heading down the hall to find our theater. (As an aside: Depriving your kids as a matter of course has its upsides. They were so thankful.)

We saw Pixar's *Brave*, something I thought we needed to do because we are rather extreme Pixar fans and we had always taken the kids when their new offerings have appeared over the years. This one just took a lot longer than usual, for some reason. (Okay, not some reason: how about $33.00 worth of reasons? Movie prices are simply obscene. Maybe I'll consider another in five years. Sorry, Hollywood. Thank God for Netflix.)

The film was very enjoyable, and exceeded my expectations. From the previews it looked like a Disney-fied feminist message movie, but I found it instead a story of conflict, estrangement, and reconciliation. They managed to cast real Scots, resulting in very authentic (if smoothed-out) accents. The obvious influence of Dunnotar Castle (an old favorite stomping-ground of ours) made it feel like home. Aside from a couple of voice-overs that tried to make the message more profound and transcendent than it really was (something about "changing your fate," when it was merely about changing a *tradition*), the story was really quite wonderful. And nothing needs to be said about the animation. It was Pixar's usual breathtaking work.

The climactic scene involves daughter Merida confessing and apologizing to her mother, whom she had deeply wronged. It was truly beautiful, yet hauntingly incomplete. There was confession: "It is all my fault." There was expression of sorrow: "I'm so sorry." There was affirmation of the relationship: "I love you."

But there was no, "Will you *forgive* me?"

I have long noticed the absence of this phrase outside of self-consciously Christian circles. The world at large contents itself with half-reconciliations. "I'm sorry," followed by, "Don't worry about it." "No problem!" "We're cool." It seems to me that the Christian worldview is unique in insisting on a full-fledged, judicial, transactional *forgiveness*. There is something, it seems, that naturally offends our sensibilities about having to say those words: "Will you forgive me?" It is an acknowledgment that somebody must bear the burden. The hurt and pain is real, and requires recompense. Real alienation cannot be smoothed over with platitudes, and maybe we just don't want to look at real alienation in the face and call it what it is. An interpersonal, "Will you forgive me?" is just loaded with transcendent echoes that we prefer not to acknowledge. For if our actions toward our fellow human beings require an active, affirmative response of forgiveness, an "I will bear the burden for your sake," and we find even that hard to accept, then what must *God* require of us?

The world knows of karma. It knows of "live and let live." It knows of "Don't worry about it." It does not know *forgiveness*. The absence of that word in the cinematic reconciliation last night was deafening in its silence. Christianity is unique in many ways, but nowhere more than in this. Only in Christianity will you find a Cross, a "crux," a place of pure alienation, a place of actual burdens borne, a fully satisfied transaction of reconciliation, an "It is finished."

In the ears of the world, Christianity is a foreign tongue. "Will you forgive me?" seems a particularly untranslatable phrase, so they've dispensed with it altogether. In truth, you need an immersion experience to truly understand it. But what a liberating immersion! Learn and know the forgiveness of God in Christ, and reconciliation with one another becomes second nature. And its absence will strike you as so incomplete you will sit in movie theaters stunned by how hollow relationships are without it.

✣ 4 ✣

IT'S THE END OF THE WORLD AS WE KNOW IT

"And I feel fine." - REM

I begin with a cultural observation, limited in scope to my own experiences. There is a major apocalyptic fever afflicting many people today, one day in advance of December 21st, 2012. Apparently, the calendar of the ancient Mayan civilization "ends" on that day, sparking the question, "What did *they* know that we don't?"

My cultural observation is that, living in the Rocky Mountain west of the United States of America, almost nobody I know of or have spoken to thinks a single thing about this curiosity. End of the world? Meh. We'll be celebrating Christmas on Tuesday. Who cares what a half-naked, pagan, Mayan scribe sitting in the jungle chiseled into a block of stone hundreds of years ago? He wasn't able to predict the demise of the Mayan civilization; why should we care about his predictions of the end of all civilization? It's been wonderful for cartoons and Internet memes, I will admit.

I have a number of Scottish friends, from my time spent in that great country. And the impression I get from reading their Facebook pages is that many in their context, and perhaps even Britain more widely, are taking the Mayan calendar curiosity very, very seriously. Many truly seem to believe that the world might end tomorrow. In their worldview, this is a distinct possibility.

~

HERE IS A COMMON NARRATIVE, so compelling it forms one of those "obvious" things everybody knows. The world before the Enlightenment should be called the "Dark Ages." It was a world of irrational superstition, desperately needing the Dawn of Reason provided by the likes of Descartes and Kant. The rise of science and reason was a fundamental break from the irrationality of the Dark Ages; never again would humanity suffer the mental disease of finding demons under every rock or suspecting witchcraft of every owner of a black cat. The world is a vast machine, ordered by unalterable physical laws; everything can be understood and known. There are no longer monsters in the closet, much less a God "up there" providentially controlling all things. The Enlightenment was the great *demystification* project. There is no more mystery. "Modern" people, scientific people, rational people are no longer captive to superstition.

~

AND YET. Mystery, it seems, is not so easy to eradicate as the materialists dream. The coldness of materialist dogma and the pretensions of its absolute claims seem to spark the opposite cultural reactions than the ones they intend. Already in the late 19th century, with the splendors of naturalistic Darwinism in full flower, Europe was, quite literally, entranced with spiritualism and the occult. Shamans and séances were commonplace and extremely popular. In 2006 two Hollywood movies were released that capture something of the fervor of the time: *The Illusionist* with Edward Norton and Paul Giamatti and *The Prestige* with Christian Bale and Hugh Jackman. The historical setting of these films is the same: late 19th century Europe. The subject of both is popular excitement with the spiritual and occult. And these films were hardly exaggera-tions. Janet Oppenheim, in her meticulously researched book, *The Other World: Spiritualism and Psychical Research in England, 1850-1914* (Cambridge, 1988) writes:

> [A] century ago, spiritualism and psychical research loomed as very serious business to some very serious and eminent people, such as the Fellows of the Royal Society, university professors, and Nobel prize-winning scientists who supported the Society for Psychical Research. Together with the industrious middle-class professionals and self-educated artisans who joined spiritualist clubs both in London and the provinces, these intellectuals turned to psychic phenomena as courageous pioneers hoping to discover the most profound secrets of the human condition and man's place in the universe [....] Their concerns and aspirations placed them—far from the lunatic fringe of their society—squarely amidst the cultural, intellectual, and emotional moods of the era. (3-4)

Few seemed particularly satisfied with the great "demystifica-tion" project. Scientists like Alfred Russel Wallace and William James were among those enamored with psychic and spiritual phenomena. Perhaps the narrative of the "Enlightenment" versus the "Dark Ages" is something more along the lines of a fairy tale.

~

THE MIDDLE AGES, too, had its share of apocalyptics, prophets, and soothsayers, particularly around the turn of the millennium: the "Chiliasts" or "millenarians." "The End is Near," read the signs, as our popular imaginations have it. And yet in the diverse "noise" of apocalyptic sentiment there was uniform structure. It was not just the "end of the world as we know it." It was *Doomsday*, or, if you prefer Chaucer's middle English, "Domesday." This was not an asteroid hitting the earth, zombies awakening to overrun cities, or the earth getting burned up by global warming. The apocalypse in the Middle Age imagination was directly linked to *the* "Apocalypse"—the Apocalypse or "Revelation" of St. John. Doomsday, the end of the world, was initiated by the return of Jesus Christ to (as the Apostles' Creed puts it) "judge the living and the dead." This was a day when all injustice would receive its just recompense, when all would be put to rights. Not an *end*, but a new beginning: the "New Heavens and the New Earth," the inauguration of God's consummation rule.

It may all seem hysterical and wild, especially at this historical vantage point: but Christian doctrine, the basic articles of the Creed, provided rather strict parameters for the apocalyptic imagination. "The End is Near" was not open-ended or devoid of content. It meant something. It meant Doomsday, the Day of Judgment. The return of the King of Kings and Lord of Lords.

Ironic. Christianity demystifies the end of the world.

∾

SCOTLAND IS A STRONGLY "POST-CHRISTIAN" society. It is commonplace to see the most beautiful churches with towering spires and stained glass windows now inhabited by nightclubs. There is one on Union Street in Aberdeen cleverly named "Soul." Scotland has moved well beyond the old "superstitions," all the nonsense about God and Jesus and the Bible and the Day of Judgment. A very grim and gritty realism characterizes its ethos. Walk along Edinburgh's Royal Mile, Aberdeen's Union Street, or visit Glasgow's Merchant City on any given night and you'll see Epicureans drinking themselves to death, for "tomorrow we die."

Yet the realism is actually *surrealism*. Divorced from the old architectonic norms of God, creation, history, providence, and judgment, people are left, quite literally, to their imaginations. Surrealism, as a philosophical school in the early 20th century, was committed to express thoughts "in the absence of all control exercised by reason, outside of all aesthetic and moral preoccupation," as one of its proponents, Andre Breton, put it.

A worldview with no boundaries, in other words.

Just as materialism spawned mysticism in the late 19th century, it does so again today. Pretend as he might, not even the great Richard Dawkins can ride to civilizational rescue now. In his *magnum opus*, *The Blind Watchmaker*, finding himself needing to explain the origins of self-replicating genes, he argued that the universe is so random, so contingent, so full of bizarre coincidences, that a marble statue of the Virgin Mary could conceivably wave at a passerby. And science was supposed to save us from superstitions.

IN UMBERTO ECO'S 1988 novel *Foucault's Pendulum*, protagonist Causabon and his companions, Belbo and Diotallevi, fabricate "The Plan," a fun and humorous game of weaving a tapestry of conspiracy from diverse materials provided by secret societies like the Knights Templar and the Rosicrucians, occultism, hermeticism, and Kabbalah. The "Plan" is basically the secret knowledge that explains the deepest mysteries of the universe. Soon they find themselves stalked by real secret society devotees who cannot be convinced that they made it all up.

Causabon finally despairs because there is no way to distinguish the truth from the lie. "The Plan" was already ludicrous, a mishmash of tendentious historical and thematic stream-of-consciousness connections. He can hardly convince his antagonists by explaining the mishmash of tendentious historical and thematic stream-of-consciousness connections. That is precisely why they believe it in the first place.

Wandering the streets of Paris, a thought occurs to panicked Causabon, a quote he cannot place at the exact moment. It turns out to be a G.K. Chesterton classic:

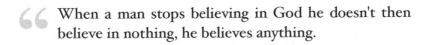 When a man stops believing in God he doesn't then believe in nothing, he believes anything.

The Enlightenment narrative has it completely wrong. And Umberto Eco, himself an atheist, was making exactly this point, once reportedly saying he fashioned the entire 600-page novel around this single Chesterton quote.

The Christian worldview or framework (God, decrees, creation, providence, meaning, purpose, judgment and end) is not the *source* of superstition. It is the bulwark *against* superstition.

Is tomorrow the End Of The World As We Know It?

I don't care. I'm a Christian.

I feel fine.

❧ 5 ☙

A VERY OLD KIND OF HERESY

A keynote address to the annual conference for truthXchange, January 2011

Good evening. Allow me to begin by expressing my deep gratitude to Peter and Rebecca Jones for their gracious invitation to address this gathering. I am honored to be here and to serve in some small way the mission of truthXchange. The topic Peter has asked me to address, "One-ism & the Gospel" is a broad one that almost begs for narrowing. This is because when one surveys the field of Protestant evangelical theology looking for areas in which, variously, pantheism, neo-paganism, or, as Peter himself has further refined it, "One-ism" has made inroads, there are any number of potential avenues to pursue.

One might perhaps immediately think of how the already weakened immune system of classic Arminian theology has been thoroughly exploited in recent years by the virus known as "Open Theism," a virus that entered right through the gaping chasm left open by a sub-biblical doctrine of God's transcendence and sovereignty. One might, alternatively, turn attention to the saccharine sweet messages of health-and-wealth preachers and note that a God conceived as one who cannot but love us is far from historical Christianity and very close to the ancient Marcionite and Gnostic notion of the divine: Jesus reveals a God of pure love far removed from the so-called "angry" God of the Old Testament. These theological trends are disturbing, to be sure. But at the outer edges of evangelicalism —and I suspect that one purpose of this conference is to question how "outer" those edges are—there is a more obvious movement that requires our attention: the so-called "Emergent" movement.

Many have been frustrated over the past decade or so in the task of evaluating the theological underpinnings and trajectories of the Emergent movement. Frustrated because, as its name suggests, the movement seems perpetually, well, *emerging*. Indeed, one of its hallmarks, held high as a badge of honor, is its lack of certainty or finality. By design it always emerges and never quite arrives. Emergent leaders have often been very vague and ambiguous when given the opportunity to render clear opinions about truths central to orthodox Christianity.

We have often been left to evaluate silences. What are we to make of someone who is crystal clear—certain, even—about God's desire for politically liberal social policies but strangely mute about, say, the deity of Christ, the atonement, sexual ethics, or the final judgment? That which used to be non-negotiable (basic doctrine) is now negotiable, and that which used to be negotiable (social policy) is now non-negotiable. We have been left to wonder what, exactly, is supposedly emerging here? I believe the answers have been reasonably clear for some time.

Nevertheless, we are thankfully no longer left to wonder. In 2010 Emergent leader Brian McLaren made the agenda clear with the publication of his book, *A New Kind of Christianity: Ten Questions That Are Transforming the Faith* (HarperCollins, 2010). As the title suggests, what is "emerging" is a new kind of Christianity. This implies, of course, that there is an old kind of Christianity that is being transformed and/or transcended, and the book leaves little doubt as to the form of Christianity meant: for McLaren, orthodox

Christianity is a dead-end that must be transcended by something new.

~

MCLAREN'S VISION for a new kind of Christianity cuts across the entire spectrum of systematic theology. There is to consider a "new" doctrine of Scripture, doctrine of God, of man, of sin, of salvation, of the church, and of the last things. Our investigation cannot thoroughly cover each of these topics, of course, so I wish to hone in on a number of key features of this "new" Christianity, each of which helps define the new Emergent gospel. I will then structure my critique around two basic questions: Is it really new? And, more importantly, is it really Christian?

I must add one more introductory note about McLaren's style and argumentative form. This will keep me from having to repeat certain frustrations as we go along. Reading Brian McLaren can be an infuriating task, but not for obvious reasons. Yes, I typically disagree with virtually every word he writes, including "and" and "the." That is not the problem. Rather, the problem is that Brian McLaren habitually adopts a wholly disingenuous posture.

On the one hand, he claims that his agenda is only to ask questions and that he has himself arrived at no settled conclusions. He is on a quest, and therefore only asks questions in search of a conversation. Yet hundreds of pages of his book are dedicated to unmitigated vitriol toward the alleged viewpoints of his theological opponents. They are, variously, warmongers, environmental polluters, capitalist exploiters uncaring about the plight of the poor, racists, homophobes, misogynists, Zionists, and religious bigots. And that is all on just one page. He believes that the traditional doctrine of God presents a "dread cosmic dictator" who is an "idol, a damnable idol [....] defended by many a well-meaning but misguided scholar and fire-breathing preacher" (65). A God who is jealous for his own name, demands exclusive loyalty, and promises final judgment is an "ugly image" of God. No settled conclusions?

Moreover, there is the frustrating fact that McLaren makes his central thesis non-falsifiable. His contention, as we will see, is that traditional Christianity is simply a dressed-up Greco-Roman worldview. But this is not the conclusion of an argument; it operates as a presupposed premise so that disagreeing invariably proves him right! The only possible explanation, it seems, for why somebody might react negatively to his rejection of, say, the unity and infallibility of the Scriptures, the Fall of humanity, the exclusivity of Christ, or the final judgment, is not a well-founded, good-faith concern, but rather that his opponent embraces the Greco-Roman worldview. He presupposes what he is supposed to be proving, and in the face of opposition he reverts to this kind of crass question-begging at every turn. This calls into question the sincerity of McLaren's desire for an honest conversation. My own critique, therefore, is not really aimed at McLaren. I offer it in the desire that we ourselves might be better equipped to know and defend "the faith once for all delivered to the saints" (Jude 3).

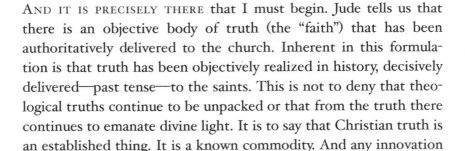

AND IT IS PRECISELY THERE that I must begin. Jude tells us that there is an objective body of truth (the "faith") that has been authoritatively delivered to the church. Inherent in this formulation is that truth has been objectively realized in history, decisively delivered—past tense—to the saints. This is not to deny that theological truths continue to be unpacked or that from the truth there continues to emanate divine light. It is to say that Christian truth is an established thing. It is a known commodity. And any innovation or new formulation must be judged according to the objective standard that has been once for all delivered to the church.

However, as far as I can see, McLaren never speaks of truth in the past tense. On the contrary, it has decidedly not been "delivered." Truth is not delivered. For McLaren, we act in hopes that the truth will be—future tense—delivered. The idea of an established, objective "truth" constrains us. Emergentism is a move away from constraints and it desires above all the freedom to question previously settled conclusions. This is, in fact, the root motivation of his entire project. He writes:

> We cry out to God, 'Please set us free!' We cry out to preachers and theologians, 'Let us go! Let us find some space to think, to worship God outside the bars and walls and fences in which we are constrained and imprisoned. We'll head out into the wilderness—risk hunger, thirst, exposure, death—but we can't sustain this constrained way of thinking, believing, and living much longer. (22)

Brian McLaren would rather die than to think, believe, and live within the boundaries of traditional Christian orthodoxy. A desire for theological autonomy is at the heart of the Emergent movement. McLaren desires an unconstrained future with no limits, no inhibitions, and full of possibility. On one level, this is simply an expected feature of his embrace of philosophical postmodernism, with its basic rejection of any sort of "foundationalism." But, as we will see, its animating power goes back a lot further than the deconstructionism of Derrida or Foucault.

McLaren believes that orthodox Christianity is a hijacked Christianity. It was born out of the civilization produced by the synthesis of Greek philosophy and the Roman political, economic, and military empire. The entire storyline of history taught by historic Christianity is not produced, he argues, by reading the Bible, but by embracing what he calls a "six-line" Greco-Roman narrative. The idea that history began in Paradise (1), went through a "Fall" (2), is now under condemnation (3), experiences salvation (4) that ultimately results in the twofold division of heaven (5) and hell (6) is a storyline that McLaren says is not morally believable. His quest, he writes, begins not by tweaking details of the conventional six-line narrative, but by calling the entire narrative scheme into question [....] We stare at this narrative, scratch our heads, and with a bewildered look ask, 'How in the world, how in God's name, could anyone ever think this is the narrative of the Bible?' (35)

Call this narrative into question, he does, beginning with its very conception of God. McLaren contrasts the God of the so-called "six-line" narrative with the true God, calling the former *Theos*, the god of the Greeks, versus *Elohim*, the God revealed in the Scriptural narrative. It is difficult to not conclude that McLaren's fundamental problem with *Theos* is that he is transcendent above his creation. In fact, not once does he refer to divine transcendence in a positive way. A God who stands outside of his creation is by that very fact, it seems, equivalent to cold, unchanging, Greek being; a sterile, Stoic, lifeless, and loveless cosmic chess-master.

Transcendence, for McLaren, appears to mean the Greek notion of "being" versus "becoming." By contrast, he asserts, the Bible tells us of the "wild, dynamic, story-unleashing goodness of Elohim." This "wild, passionate, creative, liberating, hope-inspiring God whose image emerges [in the biblical narrative] is not the dread cosmic dictator of the six-line Greco-Roman framework." One must choose between these two masters, according to McLaren: "You can try to hybridize them and compromise them for centuries, but like oil and water they eventually separate and prove incompatible. They refuse to alloy" (65).

So this is the stark choice: a God who, as Herman Bavinck helpfully puts it, "has a free, independent existence and life of his own," (whom McLaren calls *Theos*) or a God who only exists in relationship to his own creative story (whom McLaren calls *Elohim*). For McLaren, God can only be conceived as in a common journey with his creation, and anything more is allegedly the abstract, cold deity of Greek philosophy. Thus, God's transcendence above his creation is practically—if not explicitly—denied, and the animating pantheistic impulse begins to emerge. God himself is wholly part of, thus one with, his own creation.

With respect to this, we should ask a question and note an irony. When did Christianity align itself with Greco-Roman philosophy? He never quite says, but in the common version of this familiar tale the alliance is laid at the feet of Constantine and the church fathers who won the day at the Council of Nicaea in A.D. 325. What seems to escape McLaren, and others who so argue, is that one of the—if not the—central motivation in articulating and guarding the doctrine of the Trinity was to avoid conceiving of God in Greek terms! It is Arianism (anti-Trinitarianism) that views God as a single, undifferentiated being, not subject to movement or change, a sterile, lifeless, transcendent monad (McLaren's *Theos*). It was precisely the doctrine of the Trinity articulated at Nicaea that viewed God as a dynamic plenitude of life in himself, an eternal *perichoresis*—interpenetration and movement—between Father, Son, and Holy Spirit. McLaren's almost illiterate reading of Christian history gets the story exactly wrong. Far from accommodating Greek philosophy, the church successfully opposed the only people around committed to Greco-Roman philosophy at the time: Arius and his followers. To put a fine point on it: the architects of Christian orthodoxy in the early centuries emphatically opposed precisely what McLaren imagines they embraced.

～

HAVING DISPENSED with the notion that God is somehow above, outside of, or transcendent above creation and history, McLaren's "dynamic" deity becomes the God of Hegel, that is, a God who is in the evolutionary process of becoming. Indeed, he calls the story of the "Fall" (which he invariably puts in scare quotes) a "compassionate coming-of-age story" for God!

Not only are Adam and Eve moving from primitive innocence to maturation, but God is also learning and maturing, as a parent does with an errant child. The so-called "Fall," in McLaren's view, is the "first stage of ascent as human beings progress from the life of hunter-gatherers to the life of agriculturalists and beyond" (50). Note well those terms: ascent and progress. In spite of admitted setbacks, history is a record of the common journey of God and man, a journey of inevitable progress through synthesis.

Whether he would admit it or not, McLaren has resurrected German philosopher G.W.F. Hegel (if he was ever dead). History thus far has had seven stages, each one likened to the higher rung of a ladder. And, he writes, "Each level resolves issues created by the previous levels, but then creates conditions and problems that must be transcended by rising to the next" (235). In other words, Hegel's well-known historic recipe: thesis, antithesis, synthesis (repeat). There was first the quest for survival, then the quest for security, for power, for independence, for individuality, for honesty, and only now we face the seventh quest: for healing, unity, liberation, and rediscovery. The problem, he thinks, is that we are all at different stages. While he, of course, is in the seventh and highest stage and his theological opponents are all further down the ladder (nothing self-serving there), he foresees still a coming eighth stage: the "ultraviolet quest for sacredness, a desire to live in a growing conscious awareness of the presence of God and the goodness of God reflected in all things. And beyond that, we can only begin to imagine what our quest might entail" (233).

And there will be more quests, because McLaren does not believe in a final "end" of history. There is no definitive moment where history ends, no "Second Coming" of Christ, certainly no separating or sorting the sheep and goats to heaven or hell, only a never-ending journey of God and creation. We are, he writes,

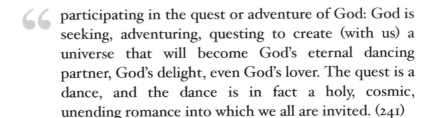

participating in the quest or adventure of God: God is seeking, adventuring, questing to create (with us) a universe that will become God's eternal dancing partner, God's delight, even God's lover. The quest is a dance, and the dance is in fact a holy, cosmic, unending romance into which we all are invited. (241)

Now, to his faint credit, McLaren realizes that he has a problem. That problem is the Bible. The Scriptures are replete with characterizations of God that cut decidedly against the grain of the purely loving, questing, adventuring God he prefers. God is presented as sovereign, a holy judge, zealous and jealous for his own name, threatening punishment and destruction to his enemies. He sometimes says and does things that are utterly abhorrent to McLaren.

There is a nifty solution, however. If God does not exist outside the narrative, then God does not speak to us from outside the narrative. That is, the Bible is not a straightforward revelation of God to us. To believe that, he asserts, is to view the Bible as a constitution, a once-for-all document that preserves or "freezes" all that is essential to know. This kind of constitutional reading is, again, allegedly a product of Greco-Roman philosophy. Instead, McLaren urges that we view the Bible as a "community library." A constitution preserves authority—and, obviously, by now you have ascertained that "authority" is a very bad word. Libraries, on the other hand, preserve a diversity of records.

The Bible, in other words, is simply the historical writings of God's people throughout their evolutionary journey. McLaren writes, "I begin to see how our ancestors' images and understandings of God continually changed, evolved, and matured over the centuries. God, it seemed, kept initiating this evolution" (99). Now, we should note for the moment that McLaren does not believe that God himself actually changed over time as if God used to be "rather adolescent, but has taken a turn for the better and is growing up nicely over the last few centuries." What he is saying is that

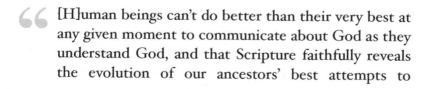

[H]uman beings can't do better than their very best at any given moment to communicate about God as they understand God, and that Scripture faithfully reveals the evolution of our ancestors' best attempts to

communicate their successive best understandings of God. As human capacity grows to conceive of a higher and wiser view of God, each new vision is faithfully preserved in Scripture like fossils in layers of sediment. (103)

Thus, we find in Scripture an evolutionary progression of human understandings of God, from a violent, tribal deity (i.e., the parts he does not like) to a "Christlike God" (i.e., the parts he does like). Now, McLaren has managed to do two momentous things at a single stroke. First, he has vindicated German philosopher Ludwig Feuerbach, who famously argued that theology is really just anthropology. When all is said and done, Christianity has been nothing more than mere men progressively projecting upward their own subjective ideals (anthropology) and imagining them to objectively apply to God (theology). This is precisely how McLaren conceives the history of revelation. Unfortunately, a man having walked this far down the road with Feuerbach might begin to have second thoughts. It might begin to dawn on him that this completely removes all possibility of knowing God at all. However much Brian McLaren wants this handy projection maneuver for only the distasteful parts of revelation, one may not walk this far with Feuerbach and turn back. The tickets sold are strictly one-way.

Second, and more disturbingly, McLaren has "re-imagined" and repackaged Marcion, the 2nd century heretic, for 21st century tastes. Marcion had similar aims. He wanted a God conceived as pure love without distasteful features like judgment, sacrifice, violence, and the like. He, likewise, knew that the Bible was a problem. So he argued that the God of the Old Testament is a different God than the Father revealed by Jesus Christ in the New Testament. This proved to be a too-radical and clumsy solution to take hold and win the day. Brian McLaren has come to the rescue with a 21st century modification. He asserts the exact same thesis—that warrants repeating. He asserts the exact same thesis, only with a much milder linguistic spin. It is not as though they really are two different Gods. It is not as though God really changed and matured over time. Rather, given the ignorance of the biblical authors throughout history, it is *as if* they are two different Gods. Which is another way of saying the differences are so stark they *might as well be* two different Gods: a violent, tribal deity versus the God of Jesus! This is a more sensitive and sophisticated presentation, surely, but there is no discernible difference.

At the risk of stating the obvious, McLaren has no room in his new kind of Christianity for Scriptural authority, since he is forced to dispense with much of it. All that is left is the echo-chamber of postmodern, emergent "conversations." Note well the way McLaren infamously dodged the uncomfortable question of homosexuality in the church: "Frankly, many of us don't know what we should think about homosexuality. We've heard all sides but no position has yet won our confidence so that we can say 'it seems good to the Holy Spirit and us.'" The answer to the question can only be found in conversation. Everything rides solely on "hearing all sides" and, not surprisingly, there is no divine voice to be heard and heeded.

~

WHAT DO we have thus far, then, in Brian McLaren's "new" kind of Christianity? It is a theology firmly resisting the allegedly suffocating constraints of historic orthodoxy. It is a theology that fundamentally denies God's transcendence, that is, that he has a "free, independent existence and life of his own." Either God is married to the world or he has no "eternal dance partner," as it were. It is a theology animated by Hegelian, evolutionary synthesis. It is a theology thoroughly post-Scripture, just as vigorously as Marcion was post-Scripture. Whereas Marcion literally cut the offending pages right out of the Bible, McLaren prefers to keep them in, if only for the nostalgic value they add to our "community library."

Finally—and fatally—McLaren's "new" kind of Christianity has no gospel. It should not surprise us that a singular emphasis on unity, oneness, progress, and synthesis should ultimately result in a world without antitheses. There is no "over-against" between God and man, Paradise and fall, covenant keepers and breakers, or heaven and hell. Not only is there no ontological antithesis between the Creator and the creature, but there is no ethical breach to be mended between a holy God and a sinful humanity. The "Fall" is but a minor setback in the evolutionary journey. It is not a cosmic crime against the Creator King, but is, rather, the "first stage of ascent." Atonement, blood, sacrifice, judgment, wrath, all these are but relics of a bygone age, the categories in which our primitive fathers happened to think.

For us this means, above all, that the Cross has no judicial significance. God's love for humanity needs not a bloody cross, atonement, or the payment of a penalty, but rather time, evolution, and progressive enlightenment. And this progressive enlightenment embraces, of course, all humanity. For McLaren there is no final judgment or hell to fear. Seemingly like all Emergent conversations, the journey never ends.

For the sake of maintaining his idea of a "loving God" he jettisons all talk of sin, wrath, and judgment. This goes to such breathtaking lengths that in his brief survey of the book of Romans, only once does Brian McLaren mention the word justification, and he never speaks of a sacrificial atonement. What a contrast to the way the Bible speaks of God's love! Paul tells us that "God demonstrates his own love for us in this: While we were still sinners, Christ died for us" (Romans 5:8). The Apostle John tells us: "This is how we know what love is: Jesus Christ laid down his life for us." (1 John 3:16). Perhaps what that means is still too obscure. So John elaborates:

 This is how God showed his love among us: He sent his one and only Son into the world that we might live through him. This is love: not that we loved God, but that he loved us and sent his Son as an atoning sacrifice for our sins (1 John 4:9-10).

Far from being inconsistent with a loving God, the bloody cross of Jesus is the very essence of God's love. And this is what the one, holy, catholic, and apostolic church has received and passed on from the beginning.

~

IS MCLAREN'S CHRISTIANITY REALLY "NEW"? Already we have witnessed the resurrection of G.W.F. Hegel, the vindication of Ludwig Feuerbach, and the Re-Imagining of Marcion. It gets more ironic.

The Emergent movement loves to tell us that their refashioning of Christianity is necessary because of the so-called "postmodern turn." In other words, they are seeking to break free from a Christianity hopelessly (so we are told) imprisoned in the clutches of Enlightenment philosophy. This is, I must say, a truly bizarre claim. For where before have we heard the theory that Christian orthodoxy is a religion hijacked by Greco-Roman philosophy?

It is so "new" that the descendants of Adolf von Harnack (1851-1930), one of the most influential Enlightenment historical critics, could probably bring a successful plagiarism case against McLaren. Nor does it take any imagination to envision Albrecht Ritschl (1822-1889) slightly peeved at the suggestion that exchanging objective, transcendent truth for a program of ethical, this-worldly social action is "new"! This is simply to say that far from being "post" modernism, McLaren has requisitioned and repackaged *modernism* at every turn. And this is not even to mention his Hegelian philosophy. One might have a lot to say about Hegelianism; that it is a new way of thinking is not one of them. It is, I dare say, the very quintessence of modernism.

At the end of the day, it is a difficult, if not impossible task to differentiate McLaren's new kind of Christianity from classic Enlightenment liberalism, the liberalism that H. Richard Niebuhr described thus: "A God without wrath brought men without sin into a kingdom without judgment through the ministrations of a Christ without a cross."

～

Is McLaren's new kind of Christianity really Christian? My convictions on the question are abundantly clear by this point, but I want to close by making one more observation. Brian McLaren is a universalist. For him, God's love is wholly indiscriminate. And all universalism, I want to suggest to you, is necessarily Gnostic, not Christian.

If one reads the Gnostic gospels uncovered after millennia in the sands of Egypt, one often encounters a repeated motif that is initially confusing. It is not enough for the ancient Gnostics to claim that the God of creation, the God of the Old Testament, is a lesser deity—actually, their characterizations are far worse: he is the bastard child of a low-level divine mistake. They insist on additionally calling Yahweh, the God of Abraham, Isaac, and Jacob an *ignorant* God. This may sound strange to our ears. Ignorant? Unknowing? Why? The explanation is both elegant and simple: The God revealed in the Old Testament Scriptures *claims to be the only God*. He actually says, "I am God, and there is no other." His ignorance, in other words, is manifest in his claim of exclusivity. It reveals his narrow narcissism that the Creator God is ignorant and unaware of the universal, all-embracing spiritual realities above even himself.

So on the one hand, we have a God who declares himself in Scripture to be the only God to whom allegiance is owed and expected. On the other hand, many claim that this cannot be true, that divine love is universal. The question is: how do they *know*? They know because they are *gnostikoi*, the "knowing ones" in touch with spiritual realities above and beyond the revelations of the ignorant Creator of heaven and earth. Yahweh may claim to be the only God, the only way, the one that must be appeased by blood and sacrifice. But they know better than he!

From this a principle follows that we would be wise to deeply internalize: all claims to universalism are necessarily claims to have access to spiritual knowledge beyond the revelation of the God of the Bible. So is it new? Is it Christian? Alas, it goes nearly all the way back. It is, in fact, humanity's very first temptation: "You will not surely die, but you will become like God, knowing good and evil." The God who made you, blesses you, makes you fruitful, is constraining you. He is lying to you. There is spiritual knowledge to be had by expanding yourselves beyond the narrow horizons of his command. Only emancipate yourself and you will become a "knowing one," a *gnostikoi*.

It may be nuanced, sophisticated—even domesticated, in fact— but Brian McLaren has declared epistemological independence from the God of Abraham, Isaac, Jacob, and Jesus, and his allegedly "new kind of Christianity" is actually the very oldest of heresies.

🦋 6 🦋

FORKED TONGUES

Five years ago my *Alma Mater*, Westminster Theological Seminary, underwent one of its greatest upheavals. Old Testament professor Peter Enns culminated a career of writing provocative journal articles by publishing an extremely controversial (and theologically poor) book explaining his views of biblical inspiration. After much campus turmoil and deliberation, the board of the seminary finally sent him on his way.

Throughout the controversy, the defense offered by Enns and his acolytes was that he was being unjustly persecuted and that, in fact, his views were solidly Reformed and evangelical. They argued that his views were fundamentally compatible with and faithful to Reformed confessions like the *Westminster Confession of Faith* and the *Three Forms of Unity*. There was nothing in his views that threatened a vital faith in the Bible. "Nothing to see here!" "No worries!" "Enns is perfectly orthodox!" was the cry. At the height of things, the board of the seminary was publicly condemned as being the "Sanhedrin" by an Enns-supporting faculty member in a chapel service.

Since his dismissal, Enns has so quickly evolved in his views that he now denies the historicity of Adam and Eve, denies that the Bible says anything about human origins, embraces theistic evolution, and denies the inerrancy and infallibility of Scripture. Which raises the question: What happened to the "Enns is perfectly Reformed and orthodox" defense? One can still argue (wrongly, in my view) that he was right; one cannot argue that his views are compatible with the Reformed confessions.

Rarely has history so quickly vindicated a controversial decision by a seminary. It is difficult to objectively examine those events and conclude anything other than that Enns and his followers were speaking with forked tongues or at least crossed fingers.

~

I RAN across a discussion on the Internet run by one of the most ardent and vocal student defenders of Enns in those days. In it he takes the full-fledged progressive view that fast food restaurant Chick-Fil-A supports "discrimination" against homosexuals, and he condemns the Christians who support the restaurant as bigoted. I am not going to litigate that issue.

What surprised me was this comment:

> You can insist all you want that you 'hate the sin but love the sinner,' but as long as you insist that a private act of love between consenting adults is an 'abomination,' and as long as millions of your fellow believers attempt to legislate against that happiness, no gay person will ever see your stance as 'love.'

What a curious statement for a professing Christian to make. You could replace that "private act of love between consenting adults" with any and every sin imaginable and arrive at the same result. Never mind that the Bible calls homosexual conduct an "abomination." Never mind that it condemns all kinds of sins. Never mind that the Apostles and missionaries of the early New Testament church, not to mention Jesus himself, had no qualms about condemning pagan idolatry and calling people to purity and holiness. Never mind that Paul actually wrote Romans chapter 1. What did all these people know?

Apparently the Apostles didn't know that calling pagans to repentance would result in a *failure of their mission*. After all, no pagan would or could see their stance as "love," right?

Never mind that the Apostolic gospel and its proclamation of repentance unto life converted practically the entire known world. This gentleman claims to know better. Christians should not insist that homosexuality or, indeed, any private behavior engaged in by "consenting adults" is sinful. Doing so is bigoted and hinders the gospel. Even more shocking, to my mind, is that he calls all of this private conduct "happiness" against which people are "legislating." *Happiness?* Perhaps someone needs to read Psalm 1 or the Beatitudes again.

I think we should seriously ask: how does one get so far afield from the Bible and its own gospel proclamation? How does a professing Christian get to the point where it is wrong to call sin *sin?* How does one promote a model of gospel witness the diametrical opposite of the Apostolic example? How does one do all this *without any apparent self-consciousness that this is happening?*

I don't know the full answer to that question. I don't know all the influences in this person's life. Clearly, the political propaganda and social agenda of the progressive left and the LGBT movement is having a substantial affect. The vocal leaders of the LGBT movement say that the gospel is offensive to them, and so this gentleman dutifully listens, lets them set the parameters of public discourse, and, on cue, sheepishly apologizes for all his embarrassing brethren who don't desist. And then he joins them in calling his brothers and sisters bigots. A sad state of affairs, really.

I am convinced, however, that a substantial part of the blame belongs to the low view of biblical inspiration this person enthusiastically imbibed in his seminary days (and "enthusiastic" is an understatement). When the "very words of God" are *reducible to* the fallible, errant words of men (essentially Enns's view), then there really is no reason to take the Bible very seriously at all. It is not an accident that those who historically have taken that view end up in theological and political liberalism. The latter is the offspring of the former.

I myself was torn about the whole situation at Westminster Seminary when all this was going on; it was ugly business any way you slice it, full of personal grudges, petty politics, and Internet litigation full of heat and no light.

After a mere five years I can say fairly confidently: the seminary did well.

7

THIS ARGUMENT HAS REACHED RETIREMENT AGE

Peter Enns has authored a new book entitled, *The Bible Tells Me So: Why Defending Scripture Has Made Us Unable to Read It* (HarperOne, 2015).

I do not care to review it. But there is one thing I can no longer do: sit idly by and let Enns continue to trot out his argument that Exodus 12:8-9 and Deuteronomy 16:5-7 contradict each other. I first heard this troubling "contradiction" from the man himself in seminary class, and he later memorialized it in his book, *Inspiration & Incarnation* (Baker Academic, 2005: 91-93). He repeats it in his latest offering.

In short: Exodus tells the Israelites to not "cook in water" (boil) the Passover lamb, but rather "roast" it over the fire.

Deuteronomy, Enns alleges, says the opposite.

Here's the relevant discrepancy:

Exodus: "do not eat the meat raw or cooked [b-sh-l] in water, but roast [ts-l-y] it over the fire."

Deuteronomy: "Boil [b-sh-l] it and eat it."

So Enns wants you to believe that Exodus says, "Don't boil the Passover lamb," and Deuteronomy says, "Boil the Passover lamb."

He has a very simple problem, however: the word b-sh-l *does not mean "boil."*

That bears repeating: The word b-sh-l *does not mean "boil."*

Now, how would I know that? I have no high expertise in biblical Hebrew. Peter Enns does. He, of all people, ought to be able to grasp the following:

The word b-sh-l in Exodus 12 is modified by a rather important prepositional phrase: *"in water."* If you want to say "boil," you add this prepositional phrase to give it the proper specificity: "cook *in water."* In other words, b-sh-l is a general term meaning, "cook." If you add "in water," voilà! You get, "boil."

Deuteronomy doesn't give the prepositional phrase. It just says, "b-sh-l and eat it." In other words, "Cook it and eat it." Not a word or hint about H_2O, water, rain, steam, precipitation, or boiling. Just, "cook it." If Deuteronomy wanted to say "boil," it would've added the necessary, "in water."

If Enns wants to argue otherwise, he can feel free to believe that in 2 Samuel 13:8 Tamar took dough, kneaded it, made cakes in the presence of Amnon, and then *boiled* (b-sh-l) them. Say what?

In sum: Exodus says "don't boil it. Roast it." Deuteronomy says, "Cook it."

∾

ENNS MAKES additional recourse to 2 Chronicles 35:13, which he takes to be evidence that the Chronicler noticed the "contradiction." It reads:

> And they roasted [b-sh-l] the Passover lamb with fire according to the rule; and they boiled [b-sh-l] the holy offerings in pots, in cauldrons, and in pans, and carried them quickly to all the lay people.

This proves my point. B-sh-l is a flexible, general, catch-all term. When you b-sh-l something with *fire*, it is called "roasting." When you b-sh-l something in *water* (per Exodus), it is called "boiling." It is a term that operates just as our English word "cook." To "cook" something is to prepare it for human consumption. It can mean any number of things, but if you want you can be more specific: "Cook it in the oven at 350 degrees." "Cook on the stovetop in a pan." "Cook in a cauldron." "Cook on the grill." And so on.

This is why Deuteronomy's, "Cook it" isn't in tension with Exodus at all. Exodus had already specified *how* (Do not "cook in water"). Interestingly, Chronicles says they "cooked it with fire *according to the rule.*" (By the way, Enns's definition would rather dubiously have this verse read: "They boiled it with fire.") The point is, Exodus was so clear the Deuteronomist didn't feel the need to specify just *how* to cook the Passover lamb, and the Chronicler feels the matter is so clear he calls it "according to the rule." There is simply no ambiguity here, much less *any* kind of tension or contradiction.

Finally, the instances of b-sh-l in the Hebrew Bible show precisely this flexibility. Sometimes it means "boil," sometimes "bake," sometimes "roast," depending on other explicitly specified contextual factors (e.g., the type of vessel being used, added elements of fire or water, etc.). When there are no such factors specified, it simply means "cook." When I say, "I'm going to cook the meat," I do not mean I'm going to *barbecue* the meat. I might mean that, but "cook" does not *mean* "barbecue." If I say, "I'm going to cook the meat *on the grill*" (oh, the wonders of the prepositional phrase!), I suddenly mean I'm going to barbecue it. I'm quite mystified that Enns doesn't get this. There's absolutely nothing to resolve.

It is time to retire this argument.

8

THE TENACITY OF THE TEXT

The other day I wrote a response to a particularly bone-headed Facebook Meme that called into question the reliability of the New Testament texts. It's a fascinating topic of study, and I didn't want to burden my readers with too much detail. But it is a worthy enough topic to follow up.

We really need to stand back and look at the big picture from time to time: the mountain of evidence for the text of the New Testament is *simply staggering*. There are around 5,700 extant manuscripts of the New Testament in various forms, from delicate fragments of papyri to the physically sturdier codices of the 4th century. On top of this, we have the extant writings of a host of early Christians: that is, people from the time period writing *about* Christianity. You know what those people do? They quote the Bible. A lot. Their quotations tell us exactly what texts they themselves were reading.

To put this into proper perspective, you must understand that scholars of antiquity generally (i.e., people working in fields not related specifically to the Bible) look at the world of New Testament scholarship with complete envy. We have exactly seven manuscripts of Plato's works. Do you know the time span between when

Plato wrote and the date of the earliest manuscript we have? 1,200 years. In other words, scholars of Greek antiquity can only dream of having the kind of textual supply that their counterparts in biblical studies have. The manuscripts that New Testament scholars routinely work with are closer to the date of textual origin by a thousand years or so.

~

AND IT ISN'T JUST one or two copies. It is hundreds and hundreds of copies from literally all over the Mediterranean world. These manuscripts do, indeed, have variants between them. Propagandists like to make that sound like a really scary thing, the assumption being that all variants are created equal. The majority of variants, for example, consist in things like this: "Jesus, our Lord," says one; "Christ Jesus, Our Lord" says another. Big deal. Right?

Well, it actually is a "deal" of sorts and so textual critics have all sorts of ways of figuring out which was the original rendering, and they're actually pretty good at it. (In that sort of case, the simpler is usually the right one, since for reasons of devotion and piety scribes would sometimes expand the references to Jesus. In other words, you could imagine a scribe adding the word "Christ," but never willfully *subtracting* it.) But no matter how you approach it there is not a single textual variant among copies of the New Testament that calls into question any major tenet of the Christian faith. That's simply a fact.

But here's something important. The diversity of the textual tradition tells us something that cuts right to the heart of the skeptics' objection. They want us to believe that *because we have so many copies* the textual tradition is uncertain and untrustworthy. Something made up, altered, or meddled with. But the reality is exactly the opposite: *because we have so many copies* the text is incapable of substantial alteration or meddling.

Here's what I mean. From the earliest times we have copies of the text from all over the known world: places like Egypt, Syria,

Turkey, and Greece. Churches would receive a letter from Paul, make copies, and send it along to other churches, who would, in turn, copy it and pass it on. The vast and rapid geographical distribution of the textual tradition means this: aside from the original recipient (and *only* the original recipient) no one person or group of people *ever* had exclusive access to the texts. (And, given the fact there's evidence Paul kept his own copies, it is unlikely that even the original recipient had exclusive access.) The likelihood of the original recipient, say, a pastor in Ephesus, changing or altering a letter from the Apostle Paul is zero. Even if he'd wanted to (I suppose Paul does teach some hard things; but if that's the case why didn't the meddler remove them?), Paul and his missionary friends were just a couple hundred miles away ministering in some other city. The truth would be quickly known.

Once the letter was copied by multiple people, the diversity of copies means it is more difficult, not less, to tamper with the text. Think of it this way: when people or organizations try to change something embarrassing on their websites, you can almost guarantee some watchdog has a "screenshot" of the original version. Or Google "cache" has preserved the original version. When the 2nd century Marcion started cutting out Bible verses and phrases he didn't like, everyone around *saw exactly what he was doing*. Why? Because everyone else had copies of the same letters, and they told a unanimous tale: Marcion was, to use Tertullian's word, "mutilating" Paul's letters.

There was never a monopoly. Never a centralized organization who possessed or had control of the texts of the New Testament. They quickly spread around the world. Nobody could substantially alter or meddle with the texts because the texts belonged to everybody. Say a lonely scribe didn't like some teaching of Paul, and left it out. There were a hundred other copies in a hundred other churches that said otherwise.

The really astonishing thing is not the variations in the texts (these were *hand* copies, after all), but rather the incredible *stability* of the text across time and space. Sometimes people call this the "tenacity" of the biblical texts. The geographical and numerical distribution of these texts makes them "stubborn" things, incredibly difficult to change. When they do get changed, it gets noticed. This is why your Bible probably has brackets around John 7:53-8:11. The textual history of that particular story is that it got inserted at some point *after* John wrote his gospel. But that's a story for another time.

Let me sum all this up for the skeptic:

The numbers, quality, antiquity, and tenacity of its text makes the New Testament arguably *the most historically reliable ancient text known to the human race.*

Skeptics who deny this are not "freethinkers" advocating enlightenment. They are literally pioneering a view that, if widely accepted, would lead us into a Dark Age of ignorance.

IS MY BABELFISH WORKING?

In his delightful and uproariously funny *Hitchhiker's Guide to the Galaxy*, Douglas Adams created the Babelfish. A tiny creature that, once introduced into the human body via the ear canal, burrows its way into the neural synapses of the brain and allows one to hear foreign languages in one's own tongue. Instant, real-time translation. It is a beautiful invention, even if only in the imagination.

I am wondering if my own Babelfish is malfunctioning and I am in need of a cranial operation to replace it.

You see, I keep reading and hearing from those in learned Christian circles that "Christendom" is dead. Not only is it dead, but it is *thankfully* dead. In the annals of bad ideas, Christendom was a very bad idea.

I suppose much depends on what one means by "Christendom." The Merriam-Webster Online Dictionary tells me that Christendom is: "The part of the world in which Christianity prevails."

That is a rather descriptive definition, and I suppose that people have in mind something a bit more prescriptive when they tell us that Christendom is a bad idea.

So let's try this: Christendom is the state of affairs in which a majority of people, societies, and cultures acknowledge, honor, and obey Jesus Christ personally, in their relationships, and in their vocations. Even that is a bit wordy, so let's just shorten it to: "Christendom is when lots of people acknowledge, honor, and obey Jesus."

You can see why I am beginning to wonder whether my instant translation has become off-kilter somehow. For when I hear learned men tell me that Christendom is a very bad thing, I am no longer hearing in my native tongue, but some strange, foreign language. My Babelfish is programmed to translate into Christian language. But this is what I'm getting:

They say: "We should not seek to establish Christendom."

I hear: "We should not seek to have lots of people acknowledge, honor, and obey Jesus."

They say: "Christendom is a failed experiment."

I hear: "Seeking to have lots of people acknowledge, honor, and obey Jesus is a failed experiment."

They say: "Jesus does not want us to establish Christendom."

I hear: "Jesus does not want lots of people to acknowledge, honor, and obey him."

They say: "Establishing Christendom is a distraction from the Church's real job."

I hear: "Seeking to have lots of people acknowledge, honor, and obey Jesus is a distraction from the Church's real job."

My Babelfish must be really malfunctioning. Because all the trendy, "in," learned Christian leaders are telling me that getting lots of people to love and serve Jesus is a very bad idea.

I've become a head case. Or have they?

❧ 10 ❧

CAN YOU TELL THE DIFFERENCE?

I recently wrote something quite provocative. I maintained that we can say with "absolute confidence" that self-anointed prophet Harold Camping does not know, and is not known by, Jesus. *Absolute confidence?* There are not too many things in this world of which we can be absolutely confident, least of which, typically, is the genuineness of another person's faith commitments. The statement either represents something resting on an unshakeable foundation, or that I am arrogant in the extreme.

I believe it is the former.

It is not as though I make it a practice to evaluate whether somebody's profession of faith in Christ is genuine. Usually, such analysis is fraught with peril, and I do not recommend it. The Harold Camping issue is, however, unique. Jesus himself expects his followers to be on the watch for false prophets—people predicting and pontificating authoritatively in the name of Jesus about matters on which Jesus has not authorized them to speak (Matt. 7:15). And the timing of his Second Coming is something about which Jesus explicitly disclaimed any knowledge (Matt. 24:36). Is the student above his Master?

Not only has Harold Camping been exposed as a false prophet, as today is now May 25th, four days beyond his prediction of Christ's return and the end of history, but the fact is that he has been exposed as such before. He once predicted the end of the world in 1994. False prophets are not "known" by Jesus, and he will not recognize them at his return. Jesus even emphasizes that this is not something ambiguous or difficult to ascertain: "I will tell them *plainly*, 'I never knew you'" (Matt. 7:23). Jesus is hearkening back to the Old Testament standard for prophets: "If what a prophet proclaims in the name of the Lord does not take place or come true, that is a message the Lord has not spoken. That prophet has spoken presumptuously. Do not be afraid of him" (Dt. 18:22). By this standard, Harold Camping is a false prophet who will stand under God's judgment. That means that whatever feelings of love and devotion he has for Jesus, they are not reciprocated. They are feelings rooted in self-deception.

So far, so clear. But this post is entitled, "Can You Tell the Difference?" What happens if the case is not so clear? What if the teaching is not something empirically falsifiable, like Camping's prediction? What if a person, in the name of Jesus, teaches something that seems to be at odds with basic biblical teaching? Can we distinguish between the true representative of God and the false?

Note very carefully: I am not yet asking *how* we tell the difference. I am asking: *can* we tell the difference? That is, are we authorized to tell the difference? The Christian community recently ran up against this question quite pointedly when a well-known Christian pastor wrote a bestselling book denying the reality of hell. A firestorm of controversy erupted, as should be expected. The one thing that filled me with more dismay than anything else was the notion, relentlessly repeated on message boards, blogs, and Facebook threads, that people are in no place to judge Rob Bell. To do so was just another example of petty, vindictive, intolerant, narrow-minded heresy hunters persecuting a brother.

Those who know me know that I have very little time for petty, vindictive, intolerant, narrow-minded heresy hunters. ("When I was a child I talked like a child, I thought like a child, I reasoned like a child. When I became a man, I put childish ways behind me." 1 Cor. 13:11). I am far from the crowd John Frame infamously named "Machen's Warrior Children," those Reformed brethren dedicated to rooting out and demolishing every theological formulation that is not a direct quote from the *Westminster Confession of Faith*.

No matter how generous of spirit I am by God's grace, however, I simply cannot, and the church simply cannot (also by God's grace) flirt with the sentiment, repeated so often about Rob Bell, that nobody is in a position to evaluate and distinguish true teaching from false. The sentiment is exactly that: just a sentiment. And pure sentiment is sentimentality. Yes, perhaps Rob Bell is sincere. Maybe he exudes a love for Jesus and others. Maybe he is "just asking questions." But if those attributes are all it takes to inoculate someone in a position of pastoral authority from scrutiny, then it follows that we simply cannot tell the difference between true and false teachers.

It is characteristic of the cultural age in which we live that sharp distinctions are purposely blurred. Postmodernism can be adequately defined in three simple words: Loss of confidence. Confidence about the truth, confidence about goodness, and confidence about beauty. That someone sees the world in "black and white" is said as a degrading slur these days. Much more laudable is a person of "nuance," who sees the world in differing shades of gray. There is always an element of truth, of course. People can be confident of the wrong things or in the wrong ways. Their "black" may not be truly black, and it is possible their "white" is just "eggshell." But that sort of nuance is not the point of our *Zeitgeist*—the spirit of our age. The point is to demolish confidence all the way down. "Who are you to judge?" Those words will be the ironic epitaph of our civilization, which seems quite determined to die on the sword of complete moral relativism.

It so happens that Jesus, unsurprisingly, provides an answer to our question: Can we tell the difference? Can we distinguish between true and false, black and white? Are we authorized to do this? Emphatically: *Yes*.

Jesus was a master of metaphor. Lilies of the field, birds of the air, mustard seeds, wheat and tares. I happen to think that his finest metaphor (If I can take the purely artistic liberty of rating them) is this one about false prophets: "They come to you in sheep's clothing, but inwardly they are ferocious wolves" (Matt. 7:15). We have heard that metaphor so often I believe we are dulled to how utterly brilliant the image is: wolves dressed as sheep. Jesus expects us to tell the difference. But it means that there will be outward similarities. There will always be things about the false teacher that people can point to: "Look at all the beautiful wool! The soft, doe-like eyes! Look how he loves the rest of the flock! He wouldn't hurt a flea!" Jesus wants his people to not be distracted by the similarities. As Little Red Riding Hood figured out, the big ears and sharp teeth are *discontinuities* that must be accounted for. The true nature of the false teacher is pure, ferocious, cold, calculating Alpha Male.

Following the sentimental reasoning of many of Rob Bell's defenders, Jesus' teaching in this regard would be nullified. For it would be impossible to detect the differences between synthetic wool and the real thing. But that is not Jesus' view of things. Most importantly, Jesus does not leave us in the dark with respect to the "how," either. He gives us a direct criterion for evaluation. Immediately after he tells us that he will not recognize the false prophets on the Day of Judgment (Matt. 7:23), he continues:

> Therefore [don't miss *that* word!-bgm] everyone who hears these words of mine and puts them into practice is like a wise man who built his house on the rock [....] But everyone who hears these words of mine and does not put them into practice is like a foolish man who built his house on sand.

What is the distinguishing criterion between wisdom and folly, truth and error, white and black? The very words of Jesus.

Jesus is continuing, amplifying, and co-opting a long Hebrew tradition of distinguishing between two distinct kinds of people.

He is directly reminiscent here of Psalm 1: Blessed is the man who "meditates on Torah day and night." Those who do not heed Torah will not "stand in the judgment." We can now get a glimpse of why Matthew tells us: "When Jesus had finished saying these things, the crowds were amazed at his teaching, because he taught as one who had authority, and not as their teachers of the law" (Matt. 7:28-29) Yes, Jesus openly identifying himself as the true Torah, the very Word of God, the very criterion between truth, wisdom, and blessedness on the one hand, and error, folly, and curse on the other hand would be rather amazing for Jewish listeners. Who does he think he is: Yahweh? Moses and the prophets pointed people to the law; Jesus points people to himself. Those who assert that Jesus never claimed to be God simply aren't reading or listening very hard.

I want to bring the point home this way: Jesus says that the measure by which we tell a true sheep from a ferocious wolf is by their fidelity to his words. Harold Camping obviously does not care about Jesus' words, for Jesus said "no one knows the day or hour," and Harold predicted both the day and the hour. Rob Bell is, at first glance, a bit of a harder case. But not really. For it is an undeniable fact that there is one person in the history of recorded humanity that spoke and taught more than anybody else about the reality of hell. That person is Jesus of Nazareth. Rob Bell is denying one thing about which Jesus was the most prolific known advocate. By definition, then, Bell is not hearing Jesus' words and putting them into practice. By definition he is engaged in folly, building a house upon the sand, and leading others to do the same.

If we listen to Jesus and put into practice what he has just taught us, then, not only can we tell the difference between a wolf and a sheep, but we can do so in this particular instance. For all the sincerity and niceness, feigned humility (always astonishing given that this is a man claiming to be wiser than nearly every other Christian teacher in history), and persuasive sentiments and words, he is an Alpha Male in the worst sense of the term: the leader of a ferocious wolf pack. It gives me no pleasure to write that. I wish it were otherwise.

In our cultural moment, the loss of confidence produced by postmodernism has had an incredibly destabilizing effect. Many have wondered the way out of our culture's relativism and lack of nerve when it comes to identifying truth, beauty, and goodness. The way out is the way Jesus identified: "*I* am the way, the truth, and the life" (John 14:6). Putting our trust in Jesus, the very Word of God made flesh, will save us not only from our sin and corruption, the Day of Judgment, and, yes, hell, but also from the sinking sands of postmodernism. For we will be building on the Rock.

Yes, we can (and must) tell the difference.

THE NECESSITY OF THE RESURRECTION

On Easter Sunday our pastor preached a fine sermon on the seminal New Testament text on the resurrection of Christ, 1 Corinthians 15, carefully following Paul's argument about the necessity of the resurrection. He pointed out the myriad terrible consequences that would result if Christ had not, indeed, been raised. Most tragically, Paul tells us, if Christ has not been raised from the dead, then we are "still in our sins."

Following the service, a very bright young man raised a question to our associate pastor that deserves serious thought and a serious answer. The question—or, more accurately, the question(s) are these: why is the resurrection necessary for the forgiveness of sins? Why isn't Jesus' suffering the penalty of sin on the cross sufficient for our salvation? Why isn't his payment of the penalty due sin sufficient to bring us into fellowship with God? It wipes out our debt, does it not? Why would we still be "in our sins" if Jesus had not been raised?

These are excellent questions. In fact, I remember a time when I myself wondered about them. I think many Christians intuitively have these questions—in fact, I know they do because my wife, who would not call herself an intellectual, has asked about these things.

~

THE FIRST THING I want to say is that these questions are, to some extent, the result of a certain kind of theological reductionism that has been present in the Western church since at least the time of St. Anselm of Canterbury. We talk all the time about the "central-ity" of the cross. We talk about the "sufficiency" of the cross. We heavily focus on the legal aspects of salvation (the doctrine of justi-fication, or being "made right" with God), and the subjective aspects of salvation (like the new birth, our internal renovation, or the doctrine of sanctification) tend to take a back seat. This gives the impression that the cross is all there is to Christianity. It does not help that the largest Christian communion in the world, the Roman Catholic Church, has as its ever-present symbol the image of Jesus hanging on the cross. Why not an empty tomb?

This is all understandable, to some degree. Does not the Apostle Paul himself say that he desires to know nothing except "Christ crucified"? But this emphasis (I do not want to say over-emphasis, for one can hardly over-emphasize the cross!) tends to obscure or push to the background other aspects of salvation that are no less important than the payment of the penalty for our sins.

In fact, sometimes it can obscure things that are right in front of our noses. For example, there is little doubt that in the doctrine of justification, the death of Christ does play a central role. Paul tells us that we can be freely justified by his grace because "God presented him as a sacrifice of atonement" (Rom. 3:25). But as we read on in Paul's exposition of the doctrine of justification by faith, it turns out that the resurrection of Christ is no less important than his sacrificial death: "[Christ] was delivered over to death for our sins and was raised to life for our justification" (Rom. 4:25). He goes on in chapter six to say, "We were therefore buried with him through baptism into death in order that, just as Christ was raised from the dead through the glory of the Father, we too may live a new life" (Rom. 6:4). In all the places, in fact, where we would go to show the centrality of the cross in Paul's thinking, we actually find the resurrection staring us right in the face. For some reason we often fail to see it.

Consider the glorious passage in Romans 8, "Therefore, there is now no condemnation for those who are in Christ Jesus [....]" The whole passage is infused with the doctrine of resurrection (e.g., vv. 11, 17, 20, 23), but most pointedly in Paul's famous question: "Who will bring any charge against those whom God has chosen?" He answers that question this way: "Christ Jesus, who died [...]" We could stop there, of course, but Paul interjects something important: "Christ Jesus, who died—more than that, who was raised to life—is at the right hand of God and is also interceding for us" (Rom. 8:33-34). My point here is that we often exaggerate Paul's emphasis on the cross as though it is to the exclusion of the empty tomb. That is not the way Paul's thinking runs. When he speaks of the cross, he has in mind the entire complex of Christ's work; he has in mind both the cross and the resurrection. For Paul, the cross without the empty tomb, a Christ who died but has not been raised to life, is utterly ineffectual for us. It leaves us, as he says, "in our sins."

~

WHOLE BOOKS COULD BE WRITTEN on this topic. In fact, they have. For one of the very best scholarly treatments I can do no better than to point you to Richard B. Gaffin Jr.'s, *Resurrection & Redemption* (P&R, 1987). For a more popular treatment, I can point you to a book written by my colleague, Andrew Sandlin: *New Flesh, New Earth: The Life-Changing Power of the Resurrection* (Oakdown, 2003).

But allow me to take a brief crack at answering these thorny questions. Let me make clear the heart of the questions: Paul claims in 1 Corinthians 15 that the resurrection was absolutely necessary for our salvation. In this he simply follows the teaching of Jesus, who often claimed that "the Son of Man must suffer many things [...] and that he must be killed and after three days rise again" (Mark 8:31). In the Greek language this is expressed with a little word, *dei*, which means "it is necessary." It has to happen. So what we are really aiming at answering is the why? What is the rationale behind that "necessity"?

The answer is supplied for us in the very context of 1 Corinthians 15. Immediately after telling us that if Christ has not been raised, we are to be pitied more than all men, Paul goes on to say:

> But Christ has indeed been raised from the dead, the firstfruits of those who have fallen asleep. For since death came through a man, the resurrection of the dead comes also through a man. For as in Adam all die, so in Christ all will be made alive. (1 Corinthians 15:20-22).

Here is the connection that will help answer our thorny questions, and it is a connection that Paul makes in a number of crucial places, particularly in Romans 5:12 and following. It is this: our destinies are indissolubly tied to an "Adam." By speaking of Christ as the "second" and "Last" Adam (1 Cor. 15:46-47), Paul is encouraging us to remember the early chapters of Genesis. These are ancient "hyperlinks." When he writes "Adam," you need to mentally click on that link and make your way back to the Garden of Eden.

There are two things that clicking on that hyperlink ought to bring to mind. First, death is the penalty threatened for Adam and Eve for disobedience. Second, there is another tree in the Garden: the tree of life, which clearly represents the opposite of death, a life of eternal freedom from sin and fellowship with God. The tree of life is important because it reminds us that the Garden of Eden was not the ultimate purpose. God had something even greater than that in mind for Adam and Eve and, by extension, all of humanity. That "something" is eternal life, free from the possibility of death.

Paul's logic, then, is that our destinies are bound up with the destiny of another: either Adam or Christ. Now, then: what benefit is a dead Christ? A dead Christ is no different from a dead Adam. They would both be under the power of death as a penalty for disobedience. And that means we too would be under the power of death. Without the resurrection, our status would not change. A dead Christ means a dead humanity, just as a dead Adam means a dead humanity. In neither case could humanity move to that place of ultimate blessing signified by the tree of life: eternal, incorruptible life.

Far too often, however, we don't think in the terms the Bible sets out for us. We think of our relationship to God as a direct, individual matter. We want to sidestep Adam (for obvious reasons), but we often want to sidestep Christ, too, as though he is only tangentially important, as though he is something of an accessory, merely an instrumental means for our forgiveness like the bulls and goats offered on the altar of old. Only by thinking this way could we have the thought that God the Father could forgive us of our sins, nullify the penalty of death, usher us into eternal life, all the while Jesus Christ, our representative, lies in a grave! It doesn't work that way. Only if Jesus is freed from the power of death can we be freed from the power of death. Only if Jesus is declared "righteous!" can we be declared righteous. Only if Jesus enters the eternal life originally promised humanity can we enter eternal life.

There is no "getting around" Jesus to get to the Father. And that really is what we're up to if we think that we can be saved while Jesus is dead. Because of Jesus' representative identity as the Second Adam, the Father can do nothing with us that he does not first do with his Son. 1 John 1:23 highlights this connection: "No one who denies the Son has the Father. Whoever confesses the Son has the Father also." The Father deals with us exclusively in his Son's representative mediation. When Jesus described himself, in other words, as the "way, the truth, and the life," he meant it. He is *the* way. There is no other place of access. When he said, "I am the resurrection and the life," he meant it. There is no other way to access eternal life than by being, as the New Testament incessantly puts it, "*in* Christ."

Much more could be said. But at very least, a dead Christ, one who lies in the grave, is no different than a dead Adam. And a dead Adam leaves us under the power of death, and so therefore does a dead Christ.

Most thankfully, however, we do not have a dead Christ, but one who has, in fact, been raised from the dead. He is the firstfruits and we are the harvest. And when the time is ripe, we look forward to sharing in the same bodily resurrection life as he:

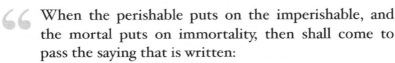

When the perishable puts on the imperishable, and the mortal puts on immortality, then shall come to pass the saying that is written:
'Death is swallowed up in victory.'
'O death, where is your victory?
O death, where is your sting?'
The sting of death is sin, and the power of sin is the law. But thanks be to God, who gives us the victory through our Lord Jesus Christ. (1 Corinthians 15:54-57)

✿ 12 ✿

DESIRE IS THE LEAST OF OUR PROBLEMS

Tiger Woods, arguably the greatest golfer of all time, just gave a lengthy statement apologizing for his multiple marital infidelities.

In that statement he acknowledges that he has practiced Buddhism throughout his life, and that his recent woes stem from abandoning Buddhism's essential principle: that *desire* is our ultimate enemy. If we could all just stop lusting, stop coveting, stop wanting and detach ourselves from the temptations that stem from desire we could enjoy happy and healthy lives. That is, in fact, the gospel according to Buddha. The ultimate source of our unhappiness is caused by desire, and the true spiritual practitioner will learn to detach himself from it.

This is not unique to Buddhism. It is part and parcel with scores of world religions. The ancient Gnostics described the "god" who created this miserable world as the "fruit of desire." What happened was that in the divine "fullness" or "pleroma" there was a defection by a spirit-being called "desire," and when she "fell" she bore a son, who, not knowing any better, created the material world, a world of lust and desire. In order to "get back" to our divine home, we must transcend and overcome this material world.

That is a mystical version of which we find a secularized counterpart in Marxism. According to Marx, all the unhappiness in the world is caused by economic inequity. That is, some people have things that others don't. If we would improve the world, we must attack this basic enemy: again, desire. If everybody has what they need, no more, no less, and nobody has more than any other, we will have vanquished the root of all evil, material (that word again!) wealth. Thus, the socialist program of eradicating inequities that cause desire.

This stems all the way back to the Garden. When Eve saw the fruit she was forbidden to eat, she saw that it "was good for food and pleasing to the eye, and also *desirable* for gaining wisdom." She took it and ate it. So does that mean the Marxists, Gnostics, and Buddhists have it right? Is desire and lust our deepest problem?

No. In fact, it is the very least of our problems. It should be noted, and deeply meditated upon, that in the Ten Commandments the one designed to address our "desire" problem is not the first. It is the last. "You shall not covet," according to God, is the last thing we need to hear, not the first. What is the first? "You shall have no other gods before me." Our fundamental, deepest problem is a *worship* problem, not a desire problem. This is the exact opposite of what the world's religions would have us believe.

PAUL EXPANDS on this in Romans 1, where the failure to worship and serve the Creator rather than the creature leads directly to "being enflamed" with ungodly *desires* (v.24). It is not the other way around. It is not that we desire and lust, and therefore stop worshiping God; it is that we stop worshiping God and therefore desire and lust.

Tiger Woods has it wrong. Television pundit Brit Hume hit the nail on the head when he said that "I think Jesus Christ offers Tiger Woods something I think Tiger Woods desperately needs." Tiger's problem does not stem from his inability to detach himself from desire. It stems from having other gods before the God who made him, gifted him and sustains him. Besides, contrary to Buddhism, Gnosticism, and Marxism, there is nothing wrong with desire in itself. There is something wrong with desiring your *neighbor's* wife, house, life, or anything else. To detach from desire is to dehumanize oneself.

Desire in itself is the very least of our problems. It is subordinate to our worship problem. The way to resolve both is to make our Tenth Commandment problem submit to the First Commandment. Tiger Woods needs, as do we, to sing this song of David:

> One thing have I desired of the Lord, this is what I seek: that I may dwell in the house of the Lord all the days of my life, to gaze upon the beauty of the Lord and to seek him in his temple. For in the day of trouble he will keep me safe in his dwelling; he will hide me in the shelter of his tabernacle and set me high upon a rock. (Psalm 27:4-5)

❧ 13 ❧

DOUBTING THOMAS

Opening remarks for a panel discussion with Dr. Francis Beckwith (Baylor University) on the topic of Thomas Aquinas and Natural Law Theory. We were each responding to a series of lectures by Dr. J. Budziszewski (University of Texas, Austin).

I am so pleased to participate in this conversation today, and I am grateful for the invitation. I also thank Professor Beckwith, whom I greatly admire, for his willingness to participate.

Our topic is Thomas Aquinas; more specifically, the viability of a revitalized natural law theory for Christian public discourse. I should admit at the outset that I am one of those Christian critics of natural law theory of whom Dr. Budziszewski has called today, "embarrassingly misinformed." But I promise I've never before let that deter me.

Let me make clear at the outset that what is in question is not that reality is ordered by transcendent norms; for me, the question is whether Thomistic natural law theory is truly capable of arriving at these norms by way of its characteristic method.

There's no better way to begin than by making the root of my concerns clear. Thomistic natural law draws a distinction (to varying degrees of sharpness) between natural knowledge and "supernatural" knowledge, between natural reason and faith, between general truths that may be known to "unaided" reason and special truths that may only be obtained by special revelation.

This is the general contour of Thomistic epistemology, and there has been great debate over just how sharply one should draw these lines. Why the concern? It is best illustrated by a philosopher who himself maximally exploited this dichotomy: Immanuel Kant. Kant famously made his distinction between faith and reason absolute: the "noumenal" realm (that which is outside our experience) is faith's domain; the phenomenal realm (the world of our experience) is reason's sole domain. It should be noted that Kant thought he was doing God a favor—"making room for him" was his phrase; but, as Stanley Fish wryly puts it, he essentially, "kicked God upstairs and out of sight."

The Enlightenment vision of Kant and his successors was to create a public space free of faith; Reason would be the sole arbiter of public truth. Insofar as natural law theory is an attempt to argue for transcendent moral norms solely on the basis of natural reason and free from faith claims, it seems content to live, move, and have its being in what I believe to be an artificial construct. I am less than inclined to accept secularism's terms of participation in the public square.

Some Thomists have felt the weight of this. Henri deLubac and the *Nouvelle Theologie* have produced a more "integrationist" account of Thomas, arguing essentially that "pure nature" is not really a condition that is unaided by God's revelation or grace after all. In fact, this more integrated interpretation is what you heard just now from Professor Beckwith, and from Dr. Budziszewski today when he insisted that, for example, without divine grace no one could reason about anything at all, or when he said that natural law takes into account the salvation history revealed in Scripture. But I have to say: Dr. Budziszewski's vigorous effort today to paint a singular, cohesive tradition of "classical natural law" genuinely surprised me. Because, with all due respect, that is embarrassingly misinformed.

Nicholas Wolterstorff, whom nobody would accuse of ignorance, summarizes in his book *Justice: Rights and Wrongs* where things stand in the scholarly world:

> To say that there is not a consensus view on Aquinas's understanding of natural law is to understate drastically the depth and scope of controversy on the matter. (Princeton, 2010: 39.)

I mention all this because I think it is important to note that there are varying accounts of Thomism, and that after these well-nigh thousand years natural law theory (still) isn't a settled matter. The irony of my disagreement just now with Dr. Budziszewski is that my own sympathies are with him and deLubac: the more integrationist an approach (meaning the *less* sharp a dichotomy between faith and reason) the better. But I also believe we do even better to rethink the entire construct.

∼

ALLOW me to briefly delve into some more specific concerns about the deployment of natural law theory.

1. I am skeptical of natural law's alleged advantage.

Here is how it appears to the popular mind: "We cannot resort to theology in matters of public concern because our opponents do not believe in theology." I hate to be the bearer of bad news, but our opponents do not believe in nature, either. These are, after all, people who believe everything—even our very biology—is a psychological and socio-cultural construct. One recent scholar has declared that mathematics is a social construct designed by white patriarchy to oppress and marginalize others. *Math.* Forgive me for pointing this out: talking about an "intrinsic teleology" or "proper ends" that we can rationally discern is every bit as unpopular with our cultured despisers as quoting John 3:16. Teleology is precisely what our culture denies.

So if public discourse requires *a priori* agreement about fundamentals like God or Nature (an impression natural law theory often gives, at least at the popular level), it strikes me that it is not in the advantageous position it imagines.

2. I am skeptical of a neat separation between general and special revelation, between the truths of reason and the truths of faith.

I find Augustine and Anselm better than Kant: knowledge—all knowledge—is "faith seeking understanding." Scratch a truth claim deep enough, and you'll uncover a faith commitment at the bottom. That's because we are dependent creatures who literally have no autonomous, independent place on which to epistemically stand.

General and special revelation should be viewed as an organic unity (not, as Thomas seemed to think, as parallel tracks) and so also the human knower must be viewed as an organic unity. People do not think in terms of two "sets" of propositions, each in a hermetically sealed silo, one called "faith" and the other "reason." Rather, they always come to topics shaped and influenced by everything they know. This is true even of natural law proponents: what they mean by their ostensibly "faith-free" references to the natural world is itself shaped by special revelation. In other words, I'm doubtful that "unaided" reason really is unaided. Try as we might to disguise it, I believe everyone's concepts of the True, Good, and Beautiful are underwritten by faith commitments.

And here's my real point: *I don't see why we should be shy or uncomfortable about this, or try to disguise it.* In his book, *The Disenchantment of Secular Discourse* (Harvard, 2010), Steven Smith compellingly shows that none of the bulwarks of our "secular" society (e.g., human dignity, equality, etc.) are arrived at by strict reason—rather, all parties smuggle their ideological faith commitments into the public square by reassuringly telling themselves and everybody else that their arguments are based on strictly "secular" reason, when they are in fact nothing of the sort.

3. I'm skeptical of natural law theory's assessment of the human epistemic condition.

I think we know what true unaided reason is. It is "futile" and "darkened," (Rom. 1) "depraved," "enslaved to the flesh," "death," "hostile to God," "unwilling" and "unable" to submit to him (Rom. 8), and "foolish" and "unspiritual" (1 Cor. 1). None of these characterizations are my own. Rather, they are how the Bible characterizes the fallen human mind. The problem is not so much that people don't believe in God; it is that they *won't* believe in God. It is a mistake to believe that human reasoning capacities are generally amenable to arguments that point in God's direction.

Now, of course unbelievers know lots of things and deploy their mental resources very successfully. I readily and thankfully admit it! After all, I'm reading this just now on a near-miraculous device created by Steve Jobs, who, as far as I know, was not on particularly close terms with God. But I think it makes a difference whether we view this general "reasonableness" as simply the natural state of affairs (a "natural law," perhaps?) or whether we view it as grace. If it is merely the natural order, we can presume upon it—indeed, so much so that we can use it, as natural law theory does, to construct a general, universal epistemology under which to do business with non-believers. But one does not presume upon grace. And grace is what I think it is.

4. I am skeptical of halfway-houses.

Don't misunderstand me: if a natural law argument persuades someone to, say, change their mind on the morality of abortion, I will rejoice. But I have doubts about an overall approach that appears satisfied with that. It seems to me one thing to not explicitly ground our foundational convictions in the Bible for a particular existential and/or situational reason (e.g., maybe quoting Scripture right now isn't the best tactic). But it seems an altogether different thing to never talk about God or his Word in public affairs *as a matter of principle*.

I am not talking about the caricature of the guy who just quotes Bible verses as "conversation stoppers." I am talking about a willingness to boldly give deep and "thick" biblical and theological descriptions of reality, to allow what we really believe to organically, openly, and unashamedly shape our entire view of Life, the Universe, and Everything. I am quite confident that can be done in conversation-enriching ways. In fact, I think it is when we actually get to the heart of the matter, the antithesis between two deep convictions on the nature of reality and ethics and knowledge, that conversations actually get interesting.

5. This one is a question:

Isn't it possible that our reluctance to engage in this kind of "thick-description" biblical and theological discourse in public affairs is one of the culprits of our cultural decline?

Why is it so easy for someone—even highly educated, lettered academics—to describe the run-of-the-mill Christian believer as a mindless "bigot"? To instinctively assume there can be no intellectual reasons for convictions brought by faith? Have not we ourselves given this very impression: reason and faith occupy two different spheres?

What if we are to blame? We have been dutifully playing by the Enlightenment's cardinal rule, "Leave God, the Bible, and your faith out of it!" Should it surprise us that we wake up to find Secularism dominating the field? I'm concerned that some versions of the natural law renewal—those that emphasize an artificial dichotomy between faith and reason—represent a doubling down on a failed strategy that got us here, rather than a real advance.

14

JUDGMENT DAY IS GOOD NEWS

Our culture is captivated with the notion that reality is meaningless and random. Science has "proven" that everything is one gigantic physical cause-and-effect machine, one damned thing after another. "Ethics" doesn't mean conforming or acting according to some universal standard to which we'll someday be held to account. No, what is important is that, at the end of the day, you were true "to yourself."

Funny thing, that phrase. True *to yourself*. The moral universe is egocentric, revolving around nothing other than *your* desires and your will. We hear it in a thousand advertisements. If it feels good, "Just Do It." Live like you're going to die young! You only live once! You deserve some "me time."

President Barack Obama once captured this moral narcissism perfectly. Asked to define sin, he said: "Being out of alignment with my values."

~

THE OTHER NIGHT I went to a movie, the new biopic of Jackie Robinson, *42*. It is quite a terrific film. I thought Harrison Ford outdid himself as Branch Rickey, the visionary owner of the Brooklyn Dodgers who bravely brought a black man to the major leagues.

Something entirely unprecedented (in my experience) occurred during the film. A number of times at the movies I have experienced the audience applauding at the end. But on this night, the crowd burst into applause in the middle of the movie.

What got them so energized? A great play? Jackie hitting a home run?

No. The prospect of Judgment Day. The notion that one day we are all going to give an account before the LORD Almighty. The idea that "sin" isn't being out of alignment with *our* values, but being out of alignment with *God's* values.

You may think I'm joking, but I am not. Every so often the Truth strikes us so powerfully it momentarily jolts us out of our make-believe, fantasy universe in which we are our own gods.

The scene is a telephone conversation between Branch Rickey and Phillies General Manager, Herb Pennock. Pennock informs Rickey that he is welcome to take the bus trip down to Philly for the upcoming series, but the Phillies wouldn't be playing the Dodgers. Herb was very clear: the Philadelphia Phillies refused to play on a baseball diamond that had a black man on it.

Branch Rickey asks Herb: "Do you think God likes baseball, Herb?"

Pennock has no idea where this is going, and says as much.

Rickey angrily shouts into the telephone:

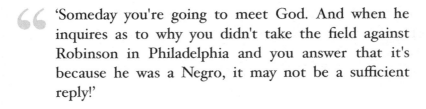

> 'Someday you're going to meet God. And when he inquires as to why you didn't take the field against Robinson in Philadelphia and you answer that it's because he was a Negro, it may not be a sufficient reply!'

As Rickey slammed down the telephone, the entire audience in the theater burst into spontaneous applause. Because everybody really knows, despite what we say, that Judgment Day is real; Judgment Day is necessary; Judgment Day is righteous. Maybe our senses are dulled in everyday life. Maybe when we're not immediately confronted with some great moral wrong we like to pretend that it's all about alignment with our own values. But this crowd couldn't help themselves; they saw Herb Pennock's ugly racism for what it was: a moral evil that needed judgment.

The real Judgment Day will be exactly like that. When the Righteous Judge starts exposing and requiting every wrong, nobody will be thinking what a jerk and a stick-in-the-mud the Judge is. They'll all be *cheering wildly*.

And the Judge is giving you an awesome grace and opportunity today, to get this urgent question answered:

What will you do when he gets to you?

15

JACK WHITE AND THE KINGDOM OF UNDERLAND

O ne of the reasons I love taking road trips is the hours it allows me to catch up on podcasts and content I never seem to get to in the hustle and bustle of daily life. The one I just had was no exception. I was listening to NPR's *All Songs Considered*, particularly Bob Boilen's interesting interview with Jack White about his new album, "Lazaretto."

Jack White, if you are unfamiliar, is difficult to describe or categorize. He is a troubadour. Poet. Guitar player. Actually, an *anything* player. If it makes sound, he plays it. Punk rocker. *Avant Garde* seems a fitting phrase. He exploded onto the scene years back with his two-piece band, *The White Stripes*. He is a visceral singer and magnetic performer.

Most of the interview with Boilen is typical banter about the craft of songwriting and recording, but it took an extraordinary turn.

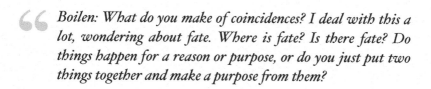 *Boilen: What do you make of coincidences? I deal with this a lot, wondering about fate. Where is fate? Is there fate? Do things happen for a reason or purpose, or do you just put two things together and make a purpose from them?*

White: Uh...
Boilen: So this is about God.
(Laughter)
White: Well, I think this is the most beautiful and the most scientifically sort of sad thing about that topic. When I was younger, you know, I had heard about synchronicity— when things are happening at the same time that means everything is going the right way.

White then shares an example of a remarkable coincidence that occurred to him regarding a 1942 penny. He continues:

> *White: But I read this article a couple years ago that scientifically, though, our brain—we have to create patterns. We look for patterns of similarity all the time.*
> *Boilen: M-m h-m-m.*
> *White: We're trying to find things that are similar so that our brains can make sense of them. And that—shockingly—is the seed for a lot of romantic ideas for a lot of people on a day-to-day basis. For a lot of artists—you know, that it was 'meant to be.' But actually it's our brain focusing on patterns trying to discover patterns all the time. And it's a little bit sad to say that—I hate even saying that out loud because it kind of kills a lot of romance about things.*

Let me pause here. This really is profound. Secularism has constructed a universe Jack White thinks he lives in, where the only thing that is "real," the only thing that "counts," is matter in motion. What is "really" happening is chemical reactions in our brains. Notice how wistful he is here for a very different kind of universe, one he wishes he lived in, one with romance, meaning, purpose, and enchantment.

And he understands the stakes. He recognizes the acid content of secular scientism: it erodes everything that makes life meaningful or worthwhile. That is why he "hates even saying that out loud."

Because it "kills a lot of romance about things." He wants to live in a romantic world, but is convinced he *really* lives in a sterile, sanitized, disenchanted world where all "meaning" is merely supplied by the wishful thinker. Boilen agrees, but he offers one, crucial caveat:

> Boilen: It does. But when those moments happen, it's really difficult to let go of the romance of it.
> White: Oh, I think we shouldn't. God, what else—we've got nothing else to talk about.

I daresay you'll not find a more haunting diagnosis of the secular condition. Resigned to our futility, knowing that life is nothing more than play-acting.

〜

"ONE WORD, MA'AM," he said, coming back from the fire; limping, because of the pain. "One word. All you've been saying is quite right, I shouldn't wonder. I'm a chap who always likes to know the worst and then put the best face I can on it. So I won't deny any of what you said. But there's one thing more to be said, even so. Suppose we have only dreamed, or made up, all those things—trees and grass and sun and moon and stars and Aslan himself. Suppose we have. Then all I can say is that, in that case, the made-up things seem a good deal more important than the real ones. Suppose this black pit of a kingdom of yours is the only world. Well, it strikes me as a pretty poor one. And that's a funny thing, when you come to think of it. We're just babies making up a game, if you're right. But four babies playing a game can make a play-world which licks your real world hollow. That's why I'm going to stand by the play-world. I'm on Aslan's side even if there isn't any Aslan to lead it. I'm going to live as like a Narnian as I can even if there isn't any Narnia. So, thanking you kindly for our supper, if these two gentlemen and the young lady are ready, we're leaving your court at once and setting out in the dark to spend our lives looking for Overland. Not that our lives will be very long, I should think; but that's a small loss if the world's as dull a *place as you say."* —Puddleglum, to the Queen of Underland, *The Silver Chair.*

MAYBE, just maybe, we should doubt all of this doubt. Maybe Jack White needs to stamp the fire the way Puddleglum did and shock himself to his senses. Maybe we don't live in the "black pit of a kingdom" secularism has constructed. Maybe there really is romance. Maybe there is meaning. Maybe there is a God who works all things for the good of those who love him and significance isn't just a chemical reaction in our heads.

If he hates "saying it out loud," he should stop believing it in his silence.

16

SCIENCE AND COGNITIVE PRIVILEGE

I want to parse a Tweet. Yes, a Tweet.

One can hardly make much of an argument in 140 characters, I admit, but sometimes brevity brings clarity.

Responding to an online interaction between philosophers Thomas Nagel and Alvin Plantinga on the epistemic failure of scientific materialism, Daniel Foster of *National Review Online* tweeted this response:

> " I'm an admirer of Nagel and Plantinga and I want scientific materialism to be false, but this is, sadly, weak stuff.

The fact that Foster finds Nagel's and Plantinga's arguments "weak stuff" does not particularly interest me. So do lots and lots of other people.

∽

No. What interests me is his stated desire that he wants scientific materialism to be false, but is having difficulty coming to that conclusion. What that implies is that Foster has, in effect, cognitively privileged scientific materialism.

A "privilege" is a "right or immunity granted as a particular benefit, advantage, or favor." The benefit, advantage, or favor being granted to scientific materialism is that it has the preeminent right to be the baseline. It is what we are to take for granted. There the edifice stands. Those who want to chip away at its foundations, men like Nagel and Plantinga, have the burden of proof, the responsibility to undermine a system that stands self-evidently and self-justifiably true. *"I want them to be right; but first they must overcome my privileged assumption that they are wrong."*

This is to miss Nagel's and Plantinga's point altogether.

Their point (a philosophically ruthless and perhaps uncomfortable one) is that scientific materialism is not entitled to privileged status at all. It is not self-evident or self-justifying, an edifice that must be taken for granted as the baseline. It is precisely this sleight-of-hand they are challenging, a sleight-of-hand so effective it has largely *produced* the widespread privileging of its construct—so widespread Dan Foster has not shaken it. It is simply not the case that scientific materialism must be taken as true and that the burden of proof must be passed on to any and all challengers.

Like Sauron and his Tower of Barad-dur, proponents of scientific materialism want you to see The Edifice, and despair. And, like Mordor, they wage a scorched-earth campaign on all challengers. The Edifice seems so imposing, its worldview so ubiquitous, they want you *not to notice* that you are cognitively privileging something that actually has nothing to recommend such a privilege.

Plantinga, Nagel, and many, many others are refusing to play that game. They are pointing to The Edifice and declaring: "A house of cards can make no demand or claim on me. It is entitled to nothing. Certainly not cognitive privilege."

Keeping with my metaphor, I think Alvin Plantinga is a real-world Tom Bombadil.

Mordor has no claim on him. Or me.

17

THE NEW GODS AND YOUR
RADIO DIAL

A crucial aspect of the worldview differences between an evangelical Christian view of things and that of progressivism is that they represent two opposing views of reality at the absolute root. Christianity understands reality, "Life, the Universe, and Everything," to have a *design*. God ordered things for the purpose of human flourishing. The cosmos has design features.

Foundational to the progressive worldview that emerged from Continental Europe in the form of German philosophy is that "God is dead." This was not a literal sort of claim, as though the Maker of Heaven and Earth had actually been killed. It is a sentiment that expresses that the Creator *hasn't existed all along.* Philosophers like Friedrich Nietzsche, G. W. F. Hegel, and Ludwig Feuerbach believed that there is no God "out there," and believing that there is has shackled humanity in primitive superstitions. Humanity has been stuck in arrested development, mentally deficient little children fantasizing about somebody greater than themselves.

By asserting that "God is dead," they meant that the old view of a Supreme Being who created and "ordered" the universe is but a figment of our imagination. What is needed is to kill off this concept of God and replace it with a far different vision: Nietzsche's "Superman," or, as Hegel put it, collective humanity embodied in the State as "God walking on the earth." If there is no God who has ordered the cosmos with built-in design features, then it is up to human beings themselves to order the universe and create the design features they desire. People need to grow up and realize that it is *they*, collectively, who are the true god.

The engine or institution through which humanity exercises these divine capacities is the State. Political observers often speak of the "Nanny State" or "Paternalism" to describe these new-found divine powers of the civil government. Government is the only providence, the only thing regulating reality and keeping you from catastrophe. It is not God who has ordered things for human flourishing; it is the State that must order things for human flourishing.

We might (and often do) find it profoundly irritating when civil governments start regulating our sugar or salt intake, banning soft drinks over 16 ounces or removing salt shakers from New York City kitchens. These may seem very small, relatively benign things. After all, is this not for the common good? I suggest that people are *mostly* right to call this phenomenon the "Nanny State" or "Paternalism." The civil government wants to protect you from yourself. Nanny doesn't want you to drink that Big Gulp. Daddy doesn't want you to have access to a salt shaker. (I'll just note that far from the usual caricature of the biblical God as an angry killjoy, he is more generous by far than his human upstarts. God has no problem with sugar and salt: he created them.)

But understanding the bigger picture, the background worldview, leads to a slightly more robust critique: this isn't a "Nanny" or a "Daddy." This is *the God-State*. City Hall, Capitol Hill, and The White House are collectively the new Mount Olympus. They are homes of gods who mingle in every single petty affair of men. We are in dire need of their intervention. Without them, we will be ignorant and obese. And, like their ancient forbears, these gods are tyrannical, capricious, and whimsical, rewarding their friends and punishing their enemies. They are mere men fancying themselves gods.

~

IT IS with that background that I have noticed a very small something recently. When driving in my car listening to the radio, I have been bombarded with radio advertisements teaching me, promising me, and warning me about the best way to live my life. I am told that I need to beware the evils of lead paint; if I don't, my children will be deaf, dumb, and blind. I am told that I need to replace all the windows in my home with "Energy Star" windows and light bulbs, which will use less electricity and save the planet. I will even be able to afford to take my kids to the state fair next year with the money I will save, so they tell me. My all-time-favorite is the radio spot telling me to wash my cutting boards and cooking surfaces. No, I am not making this up. Apparently there are vast numbers of sentient human beings living in 21st century America who do not know about bacteria.

What do all these radio spots have in common?

They all give out sponsoring Internet addresses that end with: "dot-gov." As in, GOV-ernment.

It might as well be "dot-GOD."

I do not wish to minimize the problems of lead paint, expensive electricity, or food poisoning. I have a problem with the State fancying itself god. Teaching, promising, and warning us from on high, the benevolent State intrudes into our kitchens and living rooms with only our best interests at heart (and not, surely, the interests of the Sierra Club or energy efficient window manufacturers).

Progressives "killed God" because they wanted to be free of that allegedly miserable and miserly killjoy.

Talk about projection. The killjoy, scolding gods of the new

Mount Olympus are hardly an improvement. They don't need Oracles to speak, because you supply the advertising money and they've got your radio dial.

18

IS THAT HORSE REGISTERED?

Shortly before his death, I attended the now-fairly-famous debate between Christopher Hitchens and his "scandalous" friend, evangelical Christian Larry Taunton, at the Babcock Theater in Billings, Montana. I wrote this the following morning.

I am pretty sure I was one of the only, if not *the* only, Christian standing in the book-signing line to meet Christopher Hitchens last night. At least it seemed to me that I was surrounded by his fan club, people deliriously happy, almost intoxicated, to meet the great Atheist Gadfly. I was eager, too, my copy of *God is Not Great: How Religion Poisons Everything* tucked under my arm. After all, I am something of an admirer of the man whom I would describe as our generation's H.L. Mencken. Witty, acerbic, occasionally insightful, and (very much like Mencken) woefully inept in really getting at the ultimate questions of Life, the Universe & Everything.

At any rate, upon meeting him, I did tell him that I was both a Christian and an admirer. I wished him all the best with his health problems, wished him a full recovery, and told him that I would pray to that effect. I figure that kindness, care, and compassion go

a lot further than the seemingly-futile efforts of trying to
reason Christopher Hitchens into the kingdom of God.

It was the Babcock Theater in Billings, Montana, a rather small-
time venue for the great public intellectual to appear. It was a
debate with Larry Taunton, a Christian apologist and president of
the Fixed Point Foundation, over the question of which kind of
society is more preferable to live in, one substantially influenced by
Christianity or one dominated by atheism?

Larry Taunton did a fine job, for his part. The debate was just
over an hour, so short it was more like an exchange of sound bites
than a debate. And when it comes to quick, witty one-liners and
sound bites, nobody can really hold a room's attention like Christopher Hitchens. That puts Larry at a decided disadvantage. Who is
not riveted and amused by Hitchens lampooning the idea that
pretty soon a "Muslim-coddling, chinless, spineless, poor-taste-in-
women philanderer" is set to become the *head of the Church of
England?*   Scintillating descriptions, and he was just getting
warmed up.

Delightful as it is to listen to skillful rhetoric, Hitchens (alas)
will never face the real problems in his worldview. A master of
misdirection, he purposely and repeatedly misses the point. It is a
point made many times in many ways, including last night, and,
once again, Hitchens managed to bury the inconvenient truth
under a barrage of witty one-liners. But no amount of witty one-
liners, no amount of pointing that scornful finger at the hypocrisies
of the faithful, can obscure the gaping disconnect at the heart of
Christopher Hitchens' worldview.

He is an eloquent advocate for the meaninglessness of all things.
There is no purpose for and no direction to the cosmos. He flatly
stated that human beings are, in essence, brutal, not-particularly-
well-evolved primates. The cosmos is, simply, full of "sound and
fury signifying nothing," as Shakespeare put it. This is the "sometimes terrifying" reality, as he says. But it is the only reality there is
and, in a slip of the tongue, he said it is our only... *hope.*

Well, now. The listener cannot help but notice: in addition to all that, there's a *mighty* high horse Christopher is riding. The horse is white. It is tall. Its name is "Righteousness." Christopher makes his living being the judge and executioner of everything hypocritical and wrong with the world. We heard, just last night, that Priests are *bad*; Iranian mullahs are *bad*; circumcision is *bad*; creationism is *bad*; Jesus is *bad*; vicarious atonement is *bad*. Bad, bad, bad, bad.... BAD! All that is *bad* must be opposed. Christianity is not just bad, it is an "evil" and "wicked" cult.

Well, in Montana we don't think much of horse thieves. So I would like to see Christopher's registration papers for that high horse he rides. Someone who believes in the meaninglessness of the cosmos and that we are just primitive primates has no business riding that horse. Primates do what primates do. Atoms collide as atoms collide. How Christopher can go from this bedrock "is" to mount the high horse of "ought" is his dirty little secret hiding in plain view. You can have sound and fury signifying nothing, or you can have a moral universe in which a high horse makes sense. You cannot coherently have both.

The horse is stolen, and Christopher Hitchens needs to prove his ownership.

19

CHRISTOPHER HITCHENS
(1949-2011)

The path to bliss abounds with many a snare;
Learning is one, and wit, however rare.
The Frenchman, first in literary fame
(Mention him, if you please. Voltaire?—The same),
With spirit, genius, eloquence supplied,
Lived long, wrote much, laugh'd heartily, and died;
The Scripture was his jest-book, whence he drew
Bon-mots to gall the Christian and the Jew;
An infidel in health, but what when sick?
Oh—then a text would touch him at the quick;
View him at Paris in his last career,
Surrounding throngs the demi-god revere;
Exalted on his pedestal of pride,
And fumed with frankincense on every side,
He begs their flattery with his latest breath,
And, smother'd in't at last, is praised to death!

Yon cottager, who weaves at her own door,
Pillow and bobbins all her little store;
Content though mean, and cheerful if not gay,
Shuffling her threads about the live-long day,
Just earns a scanty pittance, and at night
Lies down secure, her heart and pocket light;
She, for her humble sphere by nature fit,
Has little understanding, and no wit,
Receives no praise; but though her lot be such
(Toilsome and indigent), she renders much;
Just knows, and knows no more, her Bible true—
A truth the brilliant Frenchman never knew;
And in that charter reads with sparkling eyes,
Her title to a treasure in the skies.
Oh, happy peasant! Oh, unhappy bard!
His the mere tinsel, hers the rich reward;
He praised perhaps for ages yet to come,
She never heard of half a mile from home:
He, lost in errors, his vain heart prefers,
She, safe in the simplicity of hers.

— WILLIAM COWPER, "TRUTH"

ENCOMIA ARE FLOWING today upon the news that the Voltaire of our generation, Christopher Hitchens, has lost his battle with esophageal cancer and passed away. Many of these tributes are excellent. Other odes to the life and personage of Hitchens do something of a disservice to the man. He appeared to have little patience for exaggerated flattery. What would he think of various inflations of personality traits which, if he in fact had them, he seemed to do his best to conceal? One would think the man were the very paragon of the virtues of kindness and respect for others, rather than the man who ridiculed and mocked in the strongest terms imaginable anything and anyone even remotely related to religious faith.

Christopher Hitchens led a wild, exciting, entertaining, full, and yet dissipating and tragic life. He was critically-acclaimed as a great public intellectual, a writer of extraordinary breadth and depth, and was by all accounts armed with an uncanny and acerbic wit. My reference to Voltaire is not incidental. Like the French poet, Hitchens was a staunch defender of the Enlightenment project; and, also like his French predecessor, he spent a great deal of effort denouncing, ridiculing, and trying to exterminate Christian faith in the world. You see, because it "poisons everything."

Hitchens rode a very high horse. He might even be remembered as the Great Denunciator. The objects of his skewering were seemingly chosen without passion or prejudice. He ripped the right; he ripped the left; he ripped fascists, communists, and God; he even famously ripped Mother Theresa. And all the while, there sat Christopher Hitchens, high up above everybody and everything, dispensing judgment.

The only authority Christopher Hitchens never questioned was his own.

The great intellectual was invited, repeatedly, the opportunity to offer his credentials for why he should be heeded. Why would anybody caught up in the chaos and randomness of a basically meaningless universe (the bedrock of his own gospel!) bother listening to moralistic lectures? Confronted with that fundamental question, he simply misdirected: Atheists can be moral, too! As if that has anything to do with anything. For all the intellectual firepower, I found Hitchens to be profoundly intellectually dishonest on the most important question: the philosophical foundations for his own judgments.

This is not to minimize his gifts. But we would do well to remember that those gifts are *gifts*. His unique abilities with the English language, his quick wit, his eye for irony—all the things people are praising today—were gifts from God. The tragedy of Christopher Hitchens is that he used those very gifts to, at every possible opportunity, spit in the face of the very One who gifted him. I am reminded of Martin Luther's rebuke of Erasmus in his *Bondage of the Will*:

> I greatly feel for you for having defiled your most beautiful and ingenious language with such vile trash; and I feel an indignation against the matter also, that such unworthy stuff should be borne about in ornaments of eloquence so rare; which is as if rubbish, or dung, should be carried in vessels of gold and silver.

That aptly sums up how I feel about Christopher Hitchens: a man who used his golden implements to haul excrement.

Much has been written of the possibility of a deathbed conversion for Hitchens. Doug Wilson's reflections on that are wonderful. I do hope that Christopher yielded to his Maker in the end. If he did not, he is not in for, as Daniel Foster absurdly writes, a "glorious surprise." That's just the kind of saccharine sentiment Hitchens himself would rightly find appalling. In the event he was wrong, Christopher certainly did not expect a glorious reception. He took Christian claims about hell way too seriously for that. Would that we Christians take it as seriously!

Cowper so eloquently highlighted the chasm between great and small, the learned and ignorant, the wisdom of the world and the foolishness of the cross.

> Oh, happy peasant! Oh, unhappy bard!
>   His the mere tinsel; hers the rich reward;
>   He praised perhaps for ages yet to come;
>   She never heard of half a mile from home.

Another unhappy bard has departed this life. I sincerely hope that, before the end, he became a "happy peasant."

20

THE SCIENTIST SHALL LIVE
BY FAITH

NPR put together a terrific half-hour debate show on Intelligent Design with Stephen C. Meyer, author of *Darwin's Doubt* (HarperOne, 2014), and Michael Ruse, philosopher of science at Florida State University.

Stephen Meyer is an exceptionally articulate advocate of his view of Intelligent Design. He demonstrates very well the *prima facie* absurdity of insisting on purely "natural" explanations of "information rich systems" (e.g., DNA). His illustrative challenge is entirely ignored by his opponent, from the start of the dialogue to the end. Meyer points out that if you enter the British Museum and look at the Rosetta Stone, with its beautiful inscriptions of three different languages, it would be utterly ridiculous to exclaim, "Wow! Look at what wind and erosion have done!"

We know that information is the product of intelligence. We have no empirical experience to the contrary. Indeed, insisting that information is possible without intelligence goes against all human experience; hardly very "scientific," is it? And yet the dominant scientific regime insists that information must have a naturalistic explanation. In fact, if you don't insist on such a naturalistic explanation (e.g., wind, erosion, mutation, natural selection) then *you're not doing science.* You're doing *religion.*

This brings me to Michael Ruse, who apparently had as his goal for the exchange to excommunicate Meyer from the polite society of "science" and to banish him to the weirdo world of "religion." Along the way, he says a few things that completely betray this purpose. Specifically, this bit, which I will break down:

> I don't think [Intelligent Design] is pseudo-science. I think it's religion, quite frankly.

A stark statement of his overall purpose: Intelligent Design is not science. In fact, it isn't even *pseudo*-science. It isn't good enough to even be a credible counterfeit, in other words. This is characteristically bombastic and cocky, the sort of thing we've become so accustomed to by the Neo-Darwinian crowd it has lost all shock value. But in the next breath he says something curious:

> Now the thing about science is there's no *a priori* necessity for being natural and not introducing supernatural causes. Newton, as we well know, did.

Translation: There is nothing in the discipline of *science* that theoretically demands, as a presupposition, a commitment to naturalism. In the first breath, we had two absolutely antithetical things: the discourse of science "over here," and the discourse of religion "over there." Naturalism belonged to the one (science) and supernaturalism, the other (religion). Never the two shall meet. In the second breath Ruse asserts that one *can* legitimately do science without a commitment to naturalism. Newton did it. (And, one might add, so did Kepler, Bacon, Copernicus, Galileo, etc.—religious nutcases, all.) Now the "camps" are becoming pretty blurred, at least as a matter of starting principles. Remember, Ruse is talking about *a priori* necessity here. It is illegitimate, in his view, to *assume at the outset* that science must be strictly naturalistic.

But if that's the case, why all the excommunication, bluster, and banishment? And how can Ruse then claim that, by simple virtue of invoking something supernatural, Stephen Meyer is guilty of doing "religion," *not science*? At first he defined science very broadly, so as to *include* the likes of Newton. Now he defines science very narrowly, so as to *exclude* the likes of Meyer.

What changed?

Not science. Michael Ruse is moving the goalposts, and he now attempts to explain why science used to include people like Isaac Newton, but does so no longer:

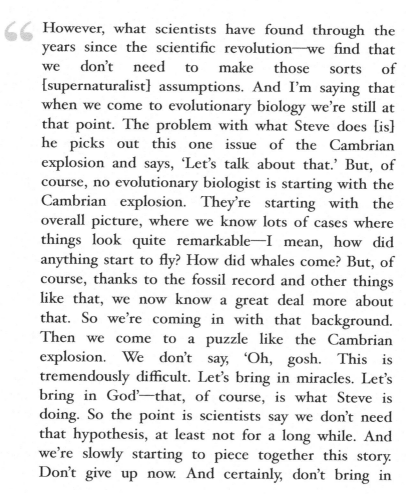

However, what scientists have found through the years since the scientific revolution—we find that we don't need to make those sorts of [supernaturalist] assumptions. And I'm saying that when we come to evolutionary biology we're still at that point. The problem with what Steve does [is] he picks out this one issue of the Cambrian explosion and says, 'Let's talk about that.' But, of course, no evolutionary biologist is starting with the Cambrian explosion. They're starting with the overall picture, where we know lots of cases where things look quite remarkable—I mean, how did anything start to fly? How did whales come? But, of course, thanks to the fossil record and other things like that, we now know a great deal more about that. So we're coming in with that background. Then we come to a puzzle like the Cambrian explosion. We don't say, 'Oh, gosh. This is tremendously difficult. Let's bring in miracles. Let's bring in God'—that, of course, is what Steve is doing. So the point is scientists say we don't need that hypothesis, at least not for a long while. And we're slowly starting to piece together this story. Don't give up now. And certainly, don't bring in

God. That's not doing science. That's not even
pseudo-science. That's religion.

Once again, he closes with maximal rhetorical flourish: *Not
science! Not even counterfeit science! Religion!* This flourish has
become something reflexive among the Neo-Darwinians, the point
of which is to distract you from looking too deeply into the matter.
Because what Michael Ruse just admitted is, given Neo-Darwinism's own rhetoric, embarrassing.

Admission One: Science=Naturalism is a *pragmatic preference
inspired by past success*. What is left unexplained is why Ruse is confident of continued future success. Some notion of the inevitability
of scientific progress is underwriting this confidence, a notion that
is not itself a product of science.

Admission Two: *Naturalism has not (as yet) explained the Cambrian
explosion*. I believe Stephen Meyer is owed an apology, frankly, at the
dismissive treatment he has received, when Ruse admits that Meyer
has, in fact, pointed to a *real*, not imaginary problem for the Neo-
Darwinian consensus.

Admission Three: *Michael Ruse lives, above all, by faith*. He is
certain that naturalism will someday, somehow, explain adequately
the problem of the Cambrian explosion. But, we must note, he has
no empirical or scientific reason to believe this.

At the end of the day, Ruse wants to define science as that
which is naturalistic because historically it has "worked." (I think
there is plenty debatable even there: finding "natural" cause and
effect in nature is not precisely the same thing as a commitment to
philosophic *naturalism*, a conflation he all-too-easily makes.) *Therefore, we must continue with pure naturalism.*

In this he assumes that because natural explanations have
worked for some (even a lot of) phenomena, it is under some kind
of compulsion or necessity to explain *all* phenomena, including the
troublesome "information rich" ones. "Certainly," he thunders,
"don't bring in *God!*" He is desperately trying to get an *a posteriori*
conclusion (it has worked) to render an *a priori* judgment (it *must*

work). He wants the "is" or "has been" to become an *ought*. It is as Lewis observed in the *Abolition of Man*:

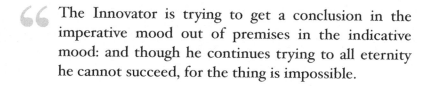 The Innovator is trying to get a conclusion in the imperative mood out of premises in the indicative mood: and though he continues trying to all eternity he cannot succeed, for the thing is impossible.

Finally, I imagine Ruse wishes to take these words back: "We don't need [the God] hypothesis, *at least not for a long while*." So he leaves open the possibility that maybe, just maybe, naturalism will fail us in the end. I have no idea who he thinks he is, decreeing for us the "time" when it will be allowable to consider a guiding intelligence.

But how *dare* Stephen Meyer explore that possibility before Michael Ruse has granted him permission?

21

(UN)INTELLIGIBLE

A great deal is happening these days in the science wars over naturalism and Intelligent Design. In addition to the NPR debate I covered between Stephen C. Meyer and Michael Ruse, Harvard psychologist Steven Pinker made a big splash in the pages of *The New Republic* (August, 2013) arguing, as his title indicates, "Science Is Not Your Enemy."

Pinker's essay is, alternatively, a denial that there exists something called "scient*ism*," and, on the other hand, that there is but it is no danger to you, your friendly college English professor, or anybody else. A more passive-aggressive approach you'll not likely encounter.

"Scientism" is what happens when the empirical sciences (which as a litmus test for membership requires the denial of transcendence) proclaim themselves the only competent arbiters of truth. As Pinker notes, this tends to ruffle the feathers of philosophers and those working in the fields once known as the humanities. (It is not an accident that they now go by the moniker "social *sciences*." You see, scientism very much does exist.)

On the one hand, Pinker declares that worries about scientism are overblown. Science is here and it means you no harm.

In the next breath, he says that science must provide the theoretical groundwork for the work of the humanities. Indeed, philosophy, history, art, language, and theology *must* listen to science for their respective disciplines to thrive. Suffice it to say, the theologian is not comforted by Pinker telling him that his discipline is okay, but first he needs to deny the existence of a transcendent God.

Did I mention passive-aggressive?

MORE SPECIFICALLY, Pinker argues that science provides two intellectual foundations that all disciplines of rational inquiry need: First, that the world is *intelligible*. The universe is "ordered." Second, that knowledge acquisition is *hard work*. No shortcuts.

Forgive me for looking askance at these benefits *science* has allegedly gifted the world. Nobody knew the universe was ordered with constant physical laws until the Enlightenment? Really? Is Pinker really unaware that science in the West flourished precisely *because* it believed the first article of the Christian creed: "I believe in God the Father Almighty, *maker of heaven and earth*"? The doctrines of creation and divine providence are nothing if not a theological affirmation (and grounding) of the uniformity of nature. Unlike pagan animism in which mysterious spiritual forces operate in matter by whim, and unlike Greek monism, which was suspicious of nature (being, after all, the creation of an evil demiurge), Christians found the world worthy of disciplined study and, well, *intelligible*. It was created by a rational mind, and is therefore rationally explicable.

I don't need to say much about science inventing the discipline of "hard work" in acquiring knowledge. Apparently Pinker has never stumbled across a copy of, say, the *Summa Theologica* or *Cur Deus Homo*? The work of lazy men, clearly.

The "intelligibility" of the cosmos was not invented by transcendence-denying Enlightenment scientists. It was borrowed by transcendence-denying Enlightenment scientists who sought, above all else, to conceal its origins in Christian theology. Like criminals sometimes file the serial numbers off their stolen pistols to obscure their origins. The guns still work, but you can't trace them back to anybody. Well, intelligibility still works, but second-hand people like Steven Pinker can blithely claim to be the original owners.

Or *does* intelligibility work, without transcendent foundations in divine providence?

I ask because I'm very familiar with one of the finest defenses of naturalistic Neo-Darwinism written in the last century: Richard Dawkins, *The Blind Watchmaker: Why the Evidence of Evolution Reveals a Universe Without Design* (Norton & Co, 1995).

That book is, if nothing else, a bold statement of the total intelligibility of the universe. In fact, it is so intelligible, Dawkins makes as his founding presupposition: "There is nothing that cannot be explained." We now have all the ingredients we need to explain literally *everything* , supplied by the laws of physics and chemistry.

Well, that's the first half of the book.

In the second half, we have chapters mulling over how to account for "information rich" systems like self-replicating DNA molecules. And Dawkins is pretty mystified. So we get dozens of pages talking about how much "luck" we are allowed in scientific hypotheses. No, I am not kidding. Dawkins says that what we need to get self-replicating DNA molecules off the ground is a fantastic "stroke of luck."

In fact, Richard Dawkins is so mystified as to the origins of DNA that he writes this sentence:

> An apparently (to ordinary human consciousness) miraculous theory is *exactly* the kind of theory we should be looking for in this particular matter of the origin of life.

Emphasis in the original.

And so he unabashedly makes recourse to his "goddess of the gaps," Lady Chance. We are allowed a certain "ration of luck," and he chooses to use his entire ration at the origins of life. And then he goes on to explain how this isn't *really* a "miracle." It is just that the universe is so old, and so random, and so weird, that certain really inexplicable things are just *bound* to happen over such long aeons of time. You thought it impossible that a marble statue of the Virgin Mary could wave at a passerby? Think again. Not impossible, just very improbable (p.159). And remember, very improbable, the "apparently miraculous" is *just what he is looking for* .

So naturalism starts out boldly proclaiming the intelligibility of the cosmos, and then boxes in the poor Neo-Darwinian into bowing down to pure, random chance by the end (or, I should say, the *beginning*).

That is not the kind of intelligibility the humanities, nor science for that matter, needs. When one of the premier naturalistic scientists of our day is telling us a marble statue can wave at somebody, something's gone off the rails.

Denial of God, who upholds and sustains the regularity and intelligibility of the cosmos, leads to folly, as the Bible reminds us time and again. In this matter, it is not the Stephen Meyers of the world looking foolish.

22

BAD SCIENCE DIES (VERY) HARD

Following up the scientific turn I have taken recently, I want to continue the theme by highlighting some very grave dangers when science becomes scient*ism*. Despite the assurances of people like Steven Pinker in his *New Republic* article that science is all about checks and balances, peer-review, open-mindedness, and discarding of discredited ideas, here in the real world the academic guild of science often believes itself impervious to critique. Paradigms gain ascendancy and then marginalize all competing hypotheses. As Thomas Kuhn showed decades ago, the process of overturning scientific consensus is a long-term affair full of intellectual, academic, and professional resistance and upheaval.

Let's be honest. Scientific orthodoxies of yesterday die hard, and some of those orthodoxies are truly horrible.

Take Thomas Malthus. He believed that resources are scarce and that there is a limit to the number of people the earth can sustain. He was the intellectual grandfather of "population control," by which I mean the forced sterilizations, abortions, and genocide carried out over the past century by bloody-minded progressive Malthusian eugenicists (and continues to this very day). Quite simply, if we don't keep the population down, we'll all starve to death.

Makes sense, doesn't it? Any Fish & Wildlife Officer out here in Montana can tell you that if you don't allow hunting, whereby the deer are thinned out, then the entire population will be at risk because of a lack of resources.

There is one significant problem. What is true of animals is, in this case, not true of humans.

Nineteenth century Englishman Henry George put the lie to Malthus this way:

> Here is the difference between the animal and the man: both the jay-hawk and the man eat chickens, but the more jay-hawks the fewer chickens, while the more men the more chickens.

Human beings are rational and creative in ways that animals are not. More population does not mean more scarcity of resources; it almost always means (where economic freedom allows) *more resources*.

Millions of people have perished because of Malthusian orthodoxy, a fact chillingly documented in Robert Zubrin's book *Merchants of Despair : Radical Environmentalists, Criminal Pseudo-Scientists, and the Fatal Cult of Antihumanism* (Encounter Books, 2013).

Malthusianism has been a failure of spectacular proportions, which is not much comfort to the multitudes of women conned into tubal ligations or forced abortions worldwide. However, so difficult is this orthodoxy to overcome that President Obama's science adviser is none other than the most famous Malthusian of them all: Paul Ehrlich. Ehrlich's 1970 book, *Population Bomb*, revitalized Malthus and led to massive population control efforts worldwide, most notably through the efforts of the United Nations. Never mind that every single one of Ehrlich's predictions proved 100% false. He even famously lost money betting on his bad predictions. This man of scientific disgrace is honored in the West Wing and scientific guild alike.

I think of another noteworthy prognosticator in 1970, biblical prophecy guru Hal Lindsey. At least when Lindsey's predictions of the end of the world in 1988 proved untrue, people by and large stopped listening to him. Ehrlich failed no less than Lindsey, but he's still revered. Chalk it up as a case where a religious "orthodoxy" (aberrant as it was) proved easier to overturn than an equally false scientific "orthodoxy." Religious folks proved more intellectually flexible than the scientific guild. Who would have thought?

I BRING this up because public pseudo-intellectuals keep repeating Malthusian claptrap. Renowned jurist Richard Posner recently published an online essay entitled, "Does the World Need More People?" His answer? "I am dubious." Underlying his entire piece is the mistaken notion that population v. resources is a zero-sum game (jayhawks v. chickens) rather than the truth: a population explosion usually means an *innovation explosion*. Even leaving this aside, I find the fact-free rumination of these supposedly "scientific" thinkers irritating in the extreme.

Here's a reality check: if the world's population lived as densely as people do in Manhattan (very dense, to be sure, but hardly unlivable), every last man, woman, and child could live in New Zealand. But, if we wanted to spread out a bit and live, say, as densely as they do in Bangladesh, we could all live comfortably in Australia.

Posner is not alone. Now revered American intellectual Wendell Berry has tossed in his two cents which, surprisingly given his reputation for profundity, are not really worth the two cents. Again there is a Malthusian presupposition: we are all fighting over scarce resources. He has a unique twist, though. For Wendell Berry, the *worst* thing that could happen is the discovery of a limitless supply of "clean" energy. If we had such a limitless resource, he writes that we would "use the world up even faster than we are using it up now." I'm inclined to think Berry just phoned his essay in, since that sentence is literally nonsensical. (Although, now that I think about it, I don't think he owns a phone.)

The Malthusian assumption always appears in those words, though: "use it up." We are just jayhawks fighting over chickens. But I can credit Berry for at least his honesty: the solution to humanity's problems is that we all need to get *poorer*: "If we want to stop the impoverishment of land and people, we ourselves must be prepared to become poorer."

I credit him for not jetting around in his Gulfstream to preach this message.

The earth does not have too many people. We have quite the opposite problem, as Jonathan Last documents in his recent book, *What to Expect When No One's Expecting* (Encounter Books, 2013). And not just the Western world. Asia, too. And we are not "running out" of anything. It is sheer fantasy that some people can look at the industrial, technological, and economic boom of the past century and see, as Berry does, nothing but current and looming disaster. On the contrary, never have so many lived so well and so long. The relevant metrics are available for study. The world has never before had so much food, so much health, so much energy, so much clean air and water—all due to the creative genius of human persons in community.

Have there been downsides? Of course there have. But the solution to those is not to be found among the Malthusians, who invariably argue that the poorest must pay for the sins of the richest: in its worst instantiations, better that the Indians or Africans starve to death or suffer from malnutrition than feed them. That is the track record of this scientific "orthodoxy" that will itself not die.

If science is so good at fact-checking, peer-reviewing, and throwing out bad hypotheses, I have just one question in response to the condescending reassurances of Steven Pinker:

Why does Paul Ehrlich have a job at all, much less as an adviser to the President of the United States of America?

23

AN ADVENT POEM

It was in a garden that the lie began
"You shall be a god, though you are a man."
In Adam and Eve we find a rotten root—
They went astray when they ate the fruit.

Like the Father of lies they sought the throne
Wanting not God's, but their glory shown.
To a Divine race they sought to give birth
Their will be done in heaven, as it is on earth.

So the Children of Men continued this boast
In the Plains of Shinar they gathered a host.
A Tower they built to establish their Name
Shouting to heaven of their power and fame.

Through long ages the same note would ring
From the mouths of Emperors, Princes, and Kings.
"We are gods!" They said with their lavish display
With their monuments of gold with feet of clay.

Philosophers claimed again and again
That we all have the spark, buried within.
Our Reason can leave us without any doubt
There's no need to turn from within to without.

Monks of the East alter this quest
In the path of the Buddha they promise us rest.
Striving and seeking will keep you afar
For why strive to be gods when you already are?

Nietzsche proclaimed that "God is dead!"
But the epitaph hardly filled him with dread.
For Deicide leaves a throne to fill
And it can be man's, by the power of will.

We fools have thought it within our might
To rise to the heights and ascend to the light.
That man should be god is always our plan
But never that God would become a man.

Every Christmas Day the lie is exposed
We are far weaker than we ever supposed.
Hear! Oh hear now the depths of our plight
That only our Maker could make it right.

Emmanuel: God With Us.

II

CULTURE

24

THE VIA MEADIA MEETS ITS
LIMITS

I have a few words for some people I very much consider "friends." I do not know any of them personally. They are all brilliant, superb writers and thinkers from whom I've benefitted greatly over the years. We are allies making common cause on many of the public issues facing our culture and society. But on the issue at the forefront right now, they seem to be *in absentia*.

First, *National Review's* Kevin Williamson considers it effrontery to suggest that support for same-sex "marriage" is fundamentally incompatible with conservatism ("Off With Their Heads!" *National Review Online:* March 25, 2013). He wants to know who gave anyone the *ex cathedra* power of defining the limits of conservatism and wonders how, for example, one might write off Jonah Goldberg as "not conservative." I will get to Goldberg in a minute.

I can sympathize slightly with Williamson's irritation at the tendency of many conservatives to quickly write off others with whom they disagree over policy issues. This is an increasing problem, particularly in the populist wing of the conservative movement. "RINO" is an acronym that far too easily passes the lips of many, in my view. I agree with him that this needs to stop.

But is making a connection between conservatism and marriage that sort of hasty, presumptuous, and insulting move? In an article taking somebody else to task for failing to make the argument, he himself provides no rationale for why conservatism and traditional marriage *aren't* linked. I'm not sure why he places the burden of proof where he does,* but it is far from obvious that one can be conservative and wholeheartedly endorse the progressive cause *de jour*.

    * Actually, I do. It makes his job easier.

What happened to William F. Buckley's standing athwart History yelling, "Stop!"? And that's history with a capital "H." Hegelian history. Progressive history. The history people have in mind when they talk about being on its "right side." It would take Clydesdale-sized blinkers or maybe even two wholly-adhered pirate eye patches to not see that same-sex marriage advocacy (as practiced by its elites, in contrast to the average person on the street) is pure ideological progressivism: evolving beyond traditional, archaic, Judeo-Christian values and launching into new, "uncharted waters," as Justice Kennedy helpfully reminded us yesterday. I have a new test for figuring out whether some proposal is basically progressive. Count how many times liberal academics, journalists, pundits, politicians, and David Letterman recommend it because it is "on the right side of History." With respect to same-sex "marriage," this is not even questionable.

Conservatism must be, by definition, about conserving something. I trust that among the things Williamson wants to conserve are the ideas, principles, and institutions that gave us Western civilization, with its liberties and prosperity. And I do not think it controversial to suggest that among the institutions absolutely integral (foundational, even) to the things he wants to conserve is the healthy nuclear family unit. I think the burden is on him to argue that the family is incidental to the sort of cultural and societal flourishing he wants to see. And given the well-documented connection between the nuclear family unit and economic prosperity, the social science data suggesting that nuclear families produce healthier citizens by far, not to mention the obvious expansion of government power when the mediating institutions of civil society are eroded, it is a burden I do not believe he can meet.

Conservatism is about recognition of reality. In Sowell's terms, there are constraints. There is a design, a "way the world works." And for human society to flourish it needs to constrain itself to what reality is, what works. Surely Williamson will agree that the indissoluble connection, say, between labor and economic reward (or, in Arthur Brooks's pithy formula, "earned success") is a built-in design feature of human nature, and that free markets are the best way to bow to that reality and thereby flourish. Now, as a theologian I'm not shy about saying this design is built in by our Creator. I think calling it natural law is a halfway house insufficiently grounded in transcendence. Regardless, we both agree that reality is what it is. There are design features for human flourishing. And one of the most obvious ones is that boy parts and girl parts go together in pairs. This is not exactly rocket science or quantum physics. The faintest familiarity with the world proves it to be true.

I simply wish to point out the quintessential progressivism involved in saying that nature is so malleable that we (as a whole society) can deny this obvious fact and successfully launch out in search of "new ways" of family formation. If Williamson agrees with this (I don't know if he does or not) then I don't think it bewildering or beyond the pale to question the solidity of his conservatism at all. He might well support and defend some second-order conservative things (and I'm very happy he does; e.g., free markets), but on the big, fundamental ontological question he'd be right there with John Lennon and the progressives, "imagining" all sorts of ontological impossibilities. And, by the way, last I checked same-sex unions producing families is still an ontological impossibility.

Moreover, I want to know what, exactly, is conservative about making public policy based on exceptions to the rule? When did that become a feature of modern conservatism? We are about to rewrite centuries of family law, nurtured in the soil of the Western legal tradition, for 3% of the population (way smaller if you consider how few gays and lesbians are actually interested in marriage or surrogacy). And this rewriting is not being done in advance. It's like that paragon of conservatism, Nancy Pelosi, said: we've got to pass the bill so that we can find out what's in it. Since when did conservatives support massive public policy shifts without a clue what the consequences would be? Answer: they don't. By *definition*, they don't. When Kevin Williamson cannot see this basic incongruity, it suggests to me we are dealing with a case of being "cool-shamed"* rather than careful, reasoned consideration.

  * *As further evidence of being "cool-shamed," I note that he includes the customary, "Gay marriage is still somewhere around No. 8,373 things I care about...." This is the sort of sentence that serves as "preemptive inoculation" from criticism. Hey, don't pick on me! I'm not an intolerant bigot!*

Williamson appeals to an article by Jonah Goldberg ("Abortion and Gay Marriage: Separate Issues" *National Review Online:* March 22, 2013). He's trying to hurt my feelings now. Because I love Jonah Goldberg. If I could marry Jonah Gold—er, maybe that's not the best quip at the moment. In the article Jonah is making a perfectly solid point: not all social issues move in the same directions. The country has become more pro-life, more pro-gun, and more pro-gay. Disparate issues, in other words, are not necessarily like Larry, Moe, and Curly: they each have their own relatively independent "careers."

But the utility of Williamson's appeal to Goldberg rests on the misguided assumption that people like me are making the "same-sex marriage isn't conservative" argument because we somehow conflate it with *other social issues like abortion.* But go back to what I just said: same-sex "marriage" isn't conservative because it alters and/or undermines something *foundational to the very society we're trying to conserve.*

Nothing about guns. Nothing about abortion. I'm not lashing traditional marriage to a "social issues" gunwale. If you want to argue that the nuclear family unit and its unique resources for citizen-formation is irrelevant to societal flourishing and has been irrelevant up to now, neither here-nor-there, will make no difference in the world, mix and match genders, moms, and dads like interchangeable parts, then it seems to be an argument that must be *made*. Stop with the *faux* outrage at people who notice the fundamentally progressive character of the claim.

～

AND, finally, I was saddened to see Walter Russell Mead throw in the towel on same-sex marriage ("Gay Marriage: From Sexual Outlaws to Sexual In-laws." *The American Interest*: March 26, 2013). Not that Mead would self-identify as a conservative; he likes to think of himself as a "radical centrist." (How one can be a "radical" centrist escapes me.) In honor of his blog title, *Via Meadia*, he attempts a sort of "middle way," acknowledging the "inevitability" of same-sex marriage and attempting to manage or sort through what to do next. Mead is an historian *par excellence*, and as I interact with just a few things in his essay, the first deals with that fact: Walter Russell Mead is an historian.

There is something missing in Mead's essay, and is missing in most essays by conservative writers throwing in the towel on the marriage issue. What is that missing thing? There is no sense of a normative perspective. There is no appeal to anything that might provide an *ought* or *should*. It only deals with the "what is." There is no, "What *should* our society do?" Only, "What *will* our society do and what will we do in response to it?" That is a characteristic way for an historian to approach the question, but it is woefully inadequate as a contribution to the public debate. There is no leadership involved at all in merely managing the results of a popular vote. By writing an essay big on the "oh well; time will tell" theme, Mead has, in effect, shown *ethics* the door.

And *showing ethics the door is a paramount progressive "virtue," to speak paradoxically.*

If there is no "ought," there is no Reality with a capital "R." There are no design features to which we should conform. If conservatives (and I'm obviously speaking beyond Mead here) want to do away with arguing over what we *ought* to do because that's kind of unpopular right now, involving as it does moral judgments, and instead spend our time tinkering with and managing whatever historical reality humanity happens to come up with next, then they've capitulated already to progressivism's bedrock conviction: the "unconstrained" vision.

Mead does have some worries about how we're going to manage the new order of things, particularly what we're going to do about religious liberty and dissent. He offers no solutions, only hopes. He hopes that gays will lay off a little and let religious people peacefully object. He hopes that preaching from Romans 1 will still be allowed. Forgive me for finding his concluding paragraph painfully naïve:

 There are going to be a lot of issues of this kind, and we predict a bright future for discrimination and First Amendment attorneys. But it seems to us overall that the best way to handle these issues is to go slow and to leave room for reflection and compromise. America, thankfully, is a pluralistic society in which many people have different points of view. It's more important that we find a way to get along than that we reach a consensus on every divisive social issue. In recognizing and protecting the rights of sexual minorities, we should not forget to honor and respect the rights of religious dissenters as well.

Maybe Walter Russell Mead, in his commitment to "radical centrism" and the "middle way," really is under the illusion that everybody is operating in good faith and wanting to "get along." Maybe he's been so long researching the past 300 years of Anglo-American dominance that he hasn't had a chance to dip into Foucault or Queer Studies literature yet.

At a minimum, he should have a conversation with President Obama's head of the Equal Employment Opportunity Commission, Chai Feldblum. When asked what we do when a conflict arises between sexual orientation and religious liberty, Ms. Feldblum (who, I repeat, runs the *EEOC*) matter-of-factly said:

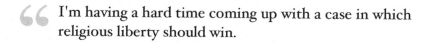 I'm having a hard time coming up with a case in which religious liberty should win.

Mr. Mead might have his hopes, but Ms. Feldblum is betting she's got the gift of prophecy.

25

THE FAMILY'S FAIR-WEATHER FRIENDS, PART ONE

The following two essays were written in response to the United States Supreme Court decision, Obergefell v. Hodges, *which legally redefined the institution of marriage to include same-sex couples.*

Reading commentary about the Supreme Court's *Obergefell v. Hodges* ruling and scrolling through my Facebook and Twitter feeds for a couple of days, at least one thing is clear to me: the institution of the family—of which orthodox Christianity is the strongest defender—is discovering it has a lot of fair-weather friends. They come in two major kinds, both disheartening. Part One will address those within the orbit of evangelical or orthodox Christianity. Part Two will address those within the politically conservative movement.

You've probably noticed the first kind already, if you have a Facebook or Twitter account. People you know, members of Bible-believing churches (if those churches even have such a thing as "membership"), professing followers of Jesus Christ, changing their profile pictures to rainbow colors and urging everybody to celebrate "love." I suspect the ranks of evangelical churches are well-nigh bursting at the seams with those who have embraced, whether by deliberate decision or—more likely—slow accommodation, the sexual ethic of our progressive age. This ethic asks two, and only two, questions: "Does it hurt anybody?" and "Is everyone treated equally?" These are strikingly *horizontal* considerations, and it might seem surprising that professing believers in, well, *God* would leave the vertical questions unasked. Surprising, that is, until you consider that a great many American Christians are actually adherents to what Notre Dame sociology professor Christian Smith coined, "Moralistic Therapeutic Deism" and aren't following the Bible or the real Jesus in the first place.

All that to say, any evangelical church that continues (or *starts*, for that matter) a wholehearted defense of the nuclear family will see its numbers shrink. The cultural climate has changed, and unpopularity—not to mention actually *obeying* Jesus' commands— isn't exactly what they bargained for. In fact, I think they're far more worried about what their friends will think than anything Jesus might think. That's what it means to be a Deist.

There is a lesser variant among this type of fair-weather friend. This is represented by the sort of man or woman (forgive my unreconstructed gender normativity) who may well support the idea of traditional marriage, be faithful followers of Jesus, but take the opportunity of recent events not to lament the moral and legal tragedy that has occurred, but to lament other Christians for pointing out, sometimes forcefully, that a moral and legal tragedy has occurred. David French describes this sort of person well:

 For many believers, this new era will present a unique challenge. Christians often strive to be seen as the "nicest" or "most loving" people in their communities. Especially among Evangelicals, there is a naïve belief that if only we were winsome enough, kind enough, and compassionate enough, the culture would welcome us with open arms. ("The Supreme Court

Ratifies a New Civic Religion That Is Incompatible With Christianity," *National Review Online*: June 26, 2015)

I'm actually sympathetic to this. Certainly there are people who panic. People consumed with anxiety and fear. People who write and talk about this as though the world is ending. Responses borne out of fear sound indistinct (as well they should) from *hatred*. I, too, lament this kind of response. We should be cheerful, kind, compassionate, and full of grace, *while we advocate for the institution of the family and the sexual ethic it involves.*

～

AH, BUT ISN'T THAT the rub? Many are those who want such advocacy to *stop*, not just that it be done in a different tone of voice. I think there are two very confused reasons for this. First, articulating biblical sexual morality involves calling sin what it actually is, among other things. And, understandably, that offends lots of people. Being "offended" in contemporary society is the apex of victimhood (so decadent are we). So in the minds of many well-intentioned people, it is axiomatic that offending someone is "unloving." For this sort of person good cheer, kindness, gentleness, compassion, and so forth are fundamentally *incompatible* with advocating a sexual ethic that offends people.

Let me just clear this up: if offending people was a sin, then Jesus of Nazareth was the chief of sinners. Not exactly where a Christian ought to be, theologically or morally speaking.

The second reason they want this advocacy to stop is that they view the institution of the family and its sexual ethic as merely "our" version of the family and sexual norms. Just one plausible hypothesis among many. After all, lots of people don't accept Christian norms about things, so who are we to enshrine them in the law? It seems rather arrogant and rude to insist that "our" private

Christian views be normative for people outside the realm of the Christian community.

One problem with this reasoning is that *someone's* understanding of human social relations is going to govern a society. There is no escaping this. The legal creation of same-sex "marriages" enthroned a dominant and governing sexual ethic in our society. If the mere fact that somebody or even lots of people don't agree with something *disqualifies* it as a public policy matter, then *Obergefell v. Hodges* has no more claim than Paul's Epistle to the Romans. I'll call myself as a witness: *I do not share its ethic.* Isn't it rather arrogant and rude for the Supreme Court to foist it on me?

Somebody will invariably respond by saying that the current law is *secular*, while "ours" is informed by religious considerations. To which I reply: first, read Justice Kennedy's decision and tell me with a straight face he doesn't have *religious* devotion to his concept of autonomy and self-actualization. If you do think his reasoning is somehow different in kind from religious dogma, explain exactly why and how. This is the sort of thing easily assumed, much more difficult to prove.

Second, the whole notion of "secular" reasoning was invented to ground morality and ethics in principles that are *universally recognized*. The whole point of the Enlightenment project was that once we all agree to the "secular" principles laid out in, say, Immanuel Kant's *Critique of Practical Reason* or John Stuart Mill's *On Liberty* everyone would lay aside their religious peculiarities and agree on everything and bloodshed and war and bigotry and ignorance and hatred and conflict would end. So, then: since we live in this secular utopia where only secular ideals govern, well-nigh 300 years on from Kant, name one issue of public policy *everybody* agrees on. Give me *one* success story. I'll wait.

Having trouble?

Of course you're having trouble, because secularism's blueprint for cultural homogeneity has been a spectacular failure. A *5-4 decision* from the Supreme Court is hardly the poster child for the promised glories of "secular" reasoning. Secular reasoning is supposed to result in 9-0 decisions, every time.* If secularism has something else going for it, some kind of "Plan B" that entitles it to rule our thoughts and societies, feel free to enlighten the rest of us.

* *In one of those once-in-a-lifetime ironies, you know what has been universally agreed upon, until about yesterday? Marriage as being between a man and a woman.*

More importantly for our fair-weather friend, what the family *is* is not "our" thing. It is not some kind of Christian distinctive. Christians *account for it* in a very specific way—as the way God designed it as recorded in Genesis 1 and 2. It is what we call a "creation ordinance," meaning that marriage is for *everybody,* Christian or not.

But even absent that theological account—and I see no good reason to leave it out—it remains what it is. Every single child born in human history (Jesus excepted) had precisely one father and one mother. This is the first human society, father+mother=children, not merely in *time,* but *priority.* It is the first society a newborn baby discovers; it remains the strongest and most foundational bond until such time as one forms another by joining with a member of the opposite sex and creating new life. It is the most visible, the most basic, and the most important of all natural human institutions. It is an anthropological and biological reality such that it is *pre*-political.

No one had to invent this society. Certainly preachers and prudes didn't invent it. Throughout all of recorded human history, all over the world, civilizations have noticed its reality, and sought to recognize and protect it as the best arrangement for social peace, prosperity, and general welfare. You know why? Because it *is* the best arrangement for social peace, prosperity, and general welfare. They noticed, among lots of things, its domesticating effects on otherwise promiscuous men, the protection it afforded otherwise vulnerable women, its stability and provision for children, its economic power, and its success as a vehicle for transmitting beliefs and values across generations.

That is the institution we are talking about. Forgive me for being irritated at those who suggest that advocating for the institution of the family is some kind of parochial defense of peculiarly Christian ideals that we have no right "imposing" on others. It is, rather, a defense of a reality that persists and survives our every attempt to circumvent it, from deadbeat dads to no-fault divorce to cohabitation. It survives because God made it, and because of a simple fact that neither you nor I, nor any homosexual or lesbian couple can escape:

Man+Woman=Children.

We've now institutionalized a version of the family where wombs must be rented and vials of sperm must be purchased. And in every case of its kind the kids will be missing one of their real parents. No one has a clue about the consequences of subjecting wombs to market valuations or embryos as economic commodities, but I guess this is one of those things Representative Nancy Pelosi would say you've got to pass so you can find out what's in it.

This much should be crystal clear: "Our" version is not the novelty. We are not the ones foisting some newfangled specialized orthodoxy on the unwilling public. There's a reason the fiat decision of five Justices of the Supreme Court was required here.

SO THE INSTITUTIONAL family has a significant constituency of fair-weather friends among evangelical and orthodox Christian communities. The first variety, the ones painting everything with rainbows, have already abandoned it. Whether they abandon their churches is simply a matter of whether their churches themselves care about the institutional family and sexual ethics. The second variety, the ones wringing their hands over the fact that other Christians take these things very seriously, are already a long way down the road of abandoning it, if for no other reason than they have accommodated the notion that offense is a sin that must be avoided at all costs. The ranks are thinning.

Obergefell was a decisive turning point and, waving the white flag, they show that their hearts were never in it. On the other hand, those of us who think that what Jesus taught is good and that history's oldest and most important institution deserves defending, will continue on unbowed. For the good of human civilization.

26

THE FAMILY'S FAIR-WEATHER FRIENDS, PART TWO

I'll begin with a proverb. Not from the Book of Proverbs. From me:

Somebody who only cares about the procedural rules by which your cause is overturned is a friend of procedural rules, not a friend of your cause.

This was blindingly obvious—truly blinding. Alliances were formed in the heat of cultural and legal battles, and it was easy to forget the basis of those alliances. Now that the smoke is clearing after the epic *Battle of Obergefell, 2015*, another sort of fair-weather friend is (or soon will be) leaving the field and issuing a hearty "good luck" to defenders of the institutional family.

It is the political ranks as much as ecclesiastical ones that are bound to thin out.

Political conservatives of a libertarian bent joined the fray, but their loyalties had little to do with what the institution of marriage ought to be. Always and ever, they stuck to their mantra with laser-like focus: "Let the states decide," or "Get the government out of it altogether." It was always about the political and judicial machinery, rarely—if ever—the substance. Although *National Review's* Kevin Williamson contributed a number of devastating salvos over the course of things, he also took offense at the notion that conservatism *requires* a defense of the family. Even the most cursory examination of the Twitter feed of another brilliant and talented member of the *National Review* squad, author of *The Conservatarian Manifesto*, Charles C.W. Cooke, reveals a man simultaneously outraged at the Supreme Court's decision and totally cool with gay marriage and even polygamy. I suppose it's possible this Tweet was a joke, but it illustrates my proverb beautifully:

> I don't care much if we get polygamy. I do care a hell of a lot about legal processes and conscience rights. #confessyourunpopularopinion

As a final exhibit, *National Review* (notice a pattern?) published a piece by Jason Lee Steorts, which argues that conservatives should *embrace* same-sex marriage ("An Equal Chance at Love," *National Review Online:* May 19, 2015). But, he is careful to say, *courts* should not be the ones to do it. All it takes to remain in the conservative fold is to focus on the procedural machinery, you see.

So the question is: what happens with these brave defenders of liberty once the *Supreme* arbiters of all things procedural render final judgment?

Surrender. And to those who don't, a great big "You're on your own now." That's what happens. They will say—well, I don't have to imagine it. *Reason's* Robby Soave already says it:

> First, to conservatives who oppose gay marriage, I say this: It's over. You lost. Please, resist the urge to die on this hill. I understand the temptation to treat the *Obergefell* ruling as merely another battle in the culture wars (like *Roe v. Wade* was) but continuing to

advocate against marriage equality risks permanently alienating the under-30 crowd. Millennials are more entrepreneurial and less loyal to the Democratic Party than most people think. Republicans (particularly libertarian-leaning Republicans) can reach them, but only if the party preaches both economic opportunity *and* social tolerance. ("Gay Marriage is Here: Now What?" *The Federalist*: June 27, 2015)

One big loss. That's all it takes to move on to the next purely procedural question—the electoral one. Don't you dare risk being unpopular with millennials, those paragons of civic wisdom! You'll ruin everything.

It is also worth observing that many politicians and pundits who, unlike Robby Soave, *are* true believers in the institutional family reflexively fell into the strictly procedural argument. One would have been justified in coming away from their analyses thinking that the only question of import with respect to *Obergefell* was the machinery of it all: states should decide, not the courts or the federal government. As though *the question itself* is neither here nor there. Look: this battle was lost and lost long ago precisely *because* the actual case for the institutional family had not been effectively made. When most* of those against same-sex marriage stopped even trying to make it, and started singing in unison about "judicial activism," it was a sure sign that we'd lost and were left grasping for whatever straws we could get.

* *One prominent exception: Heritage Foundation's Ryan T. Anderson was unwavering in making the procedural point, but in every public appearance he always made a positive anthropological, biological, and social case for marriage as between one man and one woman. His courage was unmatched.*

∾

ALL THAT TO SAY, the political coalition around the issue of marriage is now bound to fracture. Those fair-weather friends whose ultimate loyalties are to political procedures and electoral maps will rush for the exits now that the tide has turned.

Before I go on to say why that's a bad thing, I need to note one more thing. I was just very hard on *National Review*, but it is only fair for me to point out these significant paragraphs in their own post-*Obergefell* official editorial:

> The majority points out how marriage has evolved over millennia—though hardly beyond recognition—and suggests it now must encompass homosexual relationships. But marriage evolved as societies and governments did—not as the result of imperious court decisions. Until the last several years, capped by this decision. This sloppy, arrogant precedent should worry even Americans who rejoice at the result.
>
> We, of course, do not: Same-sex marriage is not a good idea by judicial fiat, *but it is not a good idea by democratic assent, either*. The majority of Americans seem to have turned on the traditional, conjugal definition of marriage, but it is the wise one—indeed, the only coherent one. ("Against Redefining Marriage —and the Republic," *National Review Online:* June 26, 2015, emphasis added.)

It's a small thing, perhaps. But it does mean a great deal that the premier journal of political conservatism went out of its way to *not just address the purely procedural matters*. Here they say, in black and white, that it is not just judicially imposed same-sex marriage that is a bad idea, but that same-sex marriage is a bad idea, period. That is a breath of fresh air, notwithstanding the rather awkward tension I imagine it exposes between the editors and their current roster of "conservatarian" writers.

~

So why is it a bad thing that a large portion of the conservative political constituency is heading for the exits? Why should we lament the departure of our fair-weather friends?

A couplet to explain:

We need them, and we're sorry to see them go;
They need us, much more than they know.

The first line is obvious. Having more people engaged in your political coalition is better than having less. I wish the libertarian-leaning conservatives felt the gravity of the issue. I wish they grasped the significance of the cultural upheaval happening right now. I also wish I could automatically renew my passport—oh, sorry. I got distracted. It just expired. Now that I think about it, that's something the small government "conservatarians" could get behind: a more efficient passport office. It's all about greasing the wheels with those guys.

It's the second line that needs explanation. Does the libertarian wing really need their totally embarrassing step-siblings: the social conservative, pro-family wing?

Let me ask another question: what is the difference between a Libertarian's view on same-sex marriage and Justice Kennedy's? *None.* Oh, they might ever so vehemently disagree on *how* the regime of same-sex marriage came to be institutionalized in America—again, the procedures—but on the matter itself, they are of one mind.

In a wholly ironic way, Libertarians are like Presbyterians, dedicated to painstakingly managing the complete demise of their respective societies, but all "decently and in order." Just so long as it happens by majority vote on a state-by-state basis according to *The Constitution of the United States of America* (Presbyterians prefer *Robert's Rules* and the *Book of Church Order*). In principle, Libertarians are all for the vision of liberty Justice Kennedy first cast in 1992's *Planned Parenthood v. Casey,* and reiterated *ad nauseam* last week in *Obergefell v. Hodges*: "At the heart of liberty is the right to define one's own concept of existence, of meaning, of the universe, and of the mystery of human life." If enough people define their own existence in the same direction, more power to them.

My problem is that many of these pundits style themselves "conservative." Now, if "conservatism" means anything, it means conserving something. What they want to conserve is the machinery, the procedures, our *form* of government. And that's not nothing; I get that, and I'm grateful for their efforts. I read these people and share their insights all the time. But when it comes to the *substance* organized by that form, they tend to be as progressive as anyone. You want to redefine a millennia-old institution that has been one of the chief causes of human dignity and happiness in the world? If you can get it done by majority vote, you're in like Flynn.*

* *Wikipedia informs me this is a slang reference to the ease with which Hollywood actor Errol Flynn seduced women. Apropos!*

So there's little *substance* to their cause. Greasing the mechanisms by which others destroy civilization does not seem much to brag about. At very least, it lays a highly dubious claim to participating in Bill Buckley's definition of conservatism: "Standing athwart History, yelling Stop!" In this case, they're yelling "Go! Decently and in order, please!" If the "conservatarians" do not find the most ancient and widespread institution of human civilization something worth conserving, they ought to reconsider the first half of the name.

They need us for one more reason: they say they *hate* Statism and out-of-control government. But is it an accident that they refer to the civil government as "Paternalistic" and the "Nanny" state? Paternalism is what you get in a society without fathers. Nannies are what you get in a society without mothers. You'd think this might clue them in to a rather important principle: *nuclear families are one of the chief means of limiting the state.* They are the foundation of civil society, a buffer zone between the individual and the raw power of the state. I have little sympathy when you're blasé about whether children should have both a father and a mother and then complain when the state inevitably becomes one or the other. It's almost like asking for it.

So the institutional family's fair-weather political friends will—foolishly—abandon the very field they ought to care about most. It is unfortunate, because we could really use their support and they could really use our convictions.

27

THE POLITICAL MACHINE NEEDS
A CULTURAL SOUL

Opening remarks for the Center For Cultural Leadership symposium held in Winchester, Virginia, November 2014.

While it certainly didn't originate with him, the late conservative firebrand Andrew Breitbart was fond of saying that "politics is downstream from culture." For far too long political conservatives operated on the opposite principle (they still do, in many ways), getting energized every other year for the next momentous election cycle while, in the meantime, the progressive left was busy making influential movies and television shows and increasing their domination in the institutional power centers of American culture: mainstream media, Hollywood, and the academy.

More recently, the indispensable Mark Steyn gave voice to this frustration:

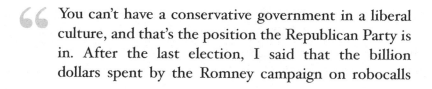 You can't have a conservative government in a liberal culture, and that's the position the Republican Party is in. After the last election, I said that the billion dollars spent by the Romney campaign on robocalls

and TV ads and all the rest had been entirely wasted, and the Electoral College breakdown would have been pretty much what it was if they'd just tossed the dough into the Potomac and let it float out to sea. But imagine the use all that money and time could have been put to out there in the wider world.

Liberals expend tremendous effort changing the culture. Conservatives expend tremendous effort changing elected officials every other November—and then are surprised that it doesn't make much difference. Culture trumps politics—which is why, once the question's been settled culturally, conservatives are reduced to playing catch-up, twisting themselves into pretzels to explain why gay marriage is really conservative after all, or why thirty million unskilled immigrants with a majority of births out of wedlock are 'natural allies' of the Republican Party. (*The Undocumented Mark Steyn*, Regnery, 2014)

Rhetorically, at least, conservatism seems to be wising up. Today, I want to explore with you the thesis that it isn't wising up by much.

While there is renewed emphasis on the need to engage "culture," the typical definition and understanding of culture strikes me as decidedly thin. What many conservatives seem to mean by engaging culture is engaging *pop* culture. We need to make more hip, cool documentaries about our policy views, a show to rival Jon Stewart's Daily Show, or alternatives to popular liberal news outlets. Pop culture is surely an aspect of culture, but it is not the same thing as culture. It is the *topmost visible layer* of culture. You can make all the wildly popular films and television shows you like, but they won't by themselves substantially change what political junkies call "the fundamentals": the subterranean, multifaceted, and broad social organism formed, maintained, and perpetuated by value-forming institutions like families, communities, churches, and education. This intricate web of institutions and voluntary associations is called "civil society," and generally speaking it is here that the character of a society is formed and fostered. Pop culture, on the other hand, is generally where the character of a society is *revealed*.

Os Guinness puts his finger on squarely on an important related problem in his recent book, *A Free People's Suicide: Sustainable Freedom and the American Future* (InterVarsity, 2012). He writes:

> [F]reedom in modern societies must be maintained and assessed at two levels, not just one: at the level of the Constitution and the structures of liberty, and at the level of the citizens and the spirit of liberty.

Guinness argues that sustainable freedom depends not only on the character of those who govern, but also the governed.

He recounts how the American founders understood that the barriers they were putting into place to curb abuses of power were mere "parchment barriers." The American system of government is not a self-perpetuating machine that would run by itself. The "nation's structures of liberty," he writes, "must always be balanced by the spirit of liberty, and the laws of the land by the habits of the heart." In other words, the "machinery" of liberty—constitutional governance—cannot adequately compensate for a loss of liberty's "spirit" in the underlying organism of society. If culture is illiberal, no amount of constitutional casuistry can save it. Simply to say, Andrew Breitbart's instincts were correct: politics is downstream from culture. The underlying intellectual and moral condition of any given citizenry will determine its political priorities.

Guinness goes on to note the deep irony that

> many educated people who scorn religious fundamentalism are hard at work creating a constitutional fundamentalism, though with lawyers and judges instead of rabbis, priests, and pastors.

> Constitutional and unconstitutional have replaced
> orthodox and heretical. But unlike the better angels of
> religious   fundamentalism,   constitutional
> fundamentalism has no recourse to a divine spirit to
> rescue it from power games, casuistry, legalism,
> litigiousness—and, eventually, calcification and death.

Here's what is deeply ironic about that: Guinness's description here does not apply, first and foremost, to progressives. In the past it applied with regularity to the social conservatives of the Moral Majority, and more recently it applies directly to Libertarians and various strains of the Tea Party movement, who seem to think that only the structures of liberty count; or at least they are more important on the priority list. Get back to constitutional, limited government, and we'll have a blessed land of liberty and justice for all. It is they who seem to believe that our system of ordered liberty is a self-perpetuating machine that works regardless of the character of the citizenry it is intended to keep free.

HERE, then, are some sobering realizations: while conservatives everywhere rhetorically champion the importance of engaging "culture," (1) they generally mean the veneer of "pop" culture, and (2) arguably two-thirds of the coalition (Libertarians and, to a lesser extent, the "Establishment") wants to do nothing of the kind. Make great movies, documentaries, and television shows, yes; address the kinds of value-laden "social" issues that comprise culture at the root level? I'll say this as clearly as I can: if you want to change culture but don't want to say a word about the erosion of marriage and the institution of the family in this country; if you want to change culture but don't want to touch the question of abortion and the sanctity of human life with a ten-foot pole; if you want to change the culture while positively championing individual ethical autonomy, you are not really interested in changing culture. You want the machinery of liberty, but not a culture that sustains liberty.

Ironically, this is a sort of mirror image of Progressivism in the early 20th century. They were the technocratic ideologues, par excellence. The elites, with armies of technical experts at their command, would organize society. It was the machinery that mattered. While the Libertarian definition of that "machinery" is antithetical to that of, say, Woodrow Wilson's, I wonder if it makes much of a difference at the end of the day?

In the 1960s Progressives wised up and realized that unless culture and civil society itself is changed, they would not succeed in their aims. And since they have advanced a long way down that road—namely, eroding civil society and replacing it with Statism—conservatives need to have something of a "Come to Jesus," moment and come to a similar realization. For the Libertarian ideal to succeed it must do exactly what Libertarianism by design cannot do—go deeper than the mere machinery of governance to address culture, what they call (with dread) "social issues."

The only thing capable of keeping government restrained and small is a virtuous civil society that is big and flourishing. This means that conservative politics cannot succeed without a conservative culture. And that means the dreaded "social issues" cannot forever be shunted to the side or evaded (as Libertarians regularly do) with abstract appeals to "Federalism" or local governance. "Let the states decide what marriage is," for example, arguably says something about the machinery of governance; it says absolutely nothing about what kind of a society conservatives are trying to conserve or achieve.

In short: culture creates politics, and wide swaths of the conservative movement are not very interested in culture. That is a pessimistic note, I grant. And since our symposium today is about pessimism, realism, and optimism, let me close by noting what I think are a few encouraging trends.

In the 2012 campaign Vice Presidential nominee Paul Ryan proved that one can address these issues in broadly appealing ways.

In a substantive speech in Cleveland, Ohio, he laid out precisely a vision for a virtuous civil society in a winsome way. Sadly, (and now for some realism) the speech got very little attention. The GOP establishment predictably didn't want to wade deeply into such waters in the heat of the Romney campaign. But the fact that a top-ticket candidate felt free and comfortable to speak in such ways is a positive sign.

Moreover, it is my sense that some of the institutions of conservatism are wising up. The Heritage Foundation and the American Enterprise Institute seem to be increasingly aware that focus cannot be solely on policy and governmental machinery, but that a vision for a virtuous civil society must be advanced. *National Review* has a solid majority of writers who regularly engage cultural and social issues. Jonathan Last of the *Weekly Standard* (author of *What to Expect When Nobody's Expecting*—how's that for dealing with a cultural issue?) has just published essays from eighteen conservative writers in a book called *The Seven Deadly Virtues* (Templeton Press, 2014), celebrating and casting a vision for the virtuous life.

These things give me hope. I believe there is a coming fracture in the conservative movement between the "social issues" faction and the Libertarian faction; and I really do think the "social issues" faction is going to win. Since the machinery of our system of ordered liberty is possible only when animated by a virtuous cultural soul, we simply have reality on our side.

28

WHAT IS A "JUST" POLITICS?

Opening remarks for the Center For Cultural Leadership annual symposium held in Saratoga, California in October, 2014.

You may well be scratching your head at the (assigned) title of my presentation: "What is a Just Politics?" From a conventional perspective it sounds like asking "What is a square circle?" or "What is a four-sided triangle?" It seems oxymoronic because politics is usually the art of compromise; it is how we organize society without killing each other. The search for purity or rectitude in politics thus seems a bit like a fool's errand—something Libertarians and certain Tea-Party types might need to reflect on.

However, justice is conformity to a standard, and the fact is that in a constitutional republic there are standards for politics, standards set forth in our foundational documents. And at a mere superficial level there are ways our politics conceivably deviates from those standards. For one example, a somewhat pressing need in our system is better protection for the integrity of our voting system. It is unconscionable that Iraq or a backwater, Stone-Age country like Afghanistan holds more transparent elections than the

United States of America. They ink-stain the fingers of people who voted. They seem actually committed to the principle of "one person, one vote." Moreover, not requiring identification to vote is a key ingredient for an "unjust" politics. Few things are more bizarre than this gaping hole in America's electoral procedure. You need identification to buy a beer or board an airplane, but not to help steer the direction of the country? It is so absurd it is no wonder the only counter-argument is to talk about the red-herring of racism. (And, incidentally: it is racist to suggest that black people are incapable of having ID.)

But those are mere procedural concerns with respect to our politics. They do erode the justice of our political system, but they are but surface issues. The more important worries are decidedly more subterranean and ideological. They clearly emerge with our current infatuation with something called "social justice."

Indeed, the rhetoric of politics in our time gives the illusion that we care deeply about justice. No proposed government action, no civic action, no corporate mission statement, is complete without affirming our commitment to something called "social justice." It's a concept so vague Jonah Goldberg's definition is probably the best we can do: Social justice is just a euphemism for "do-goodery." It is an "empty vessel to be filled with any and all leftist ideals, and then promptly wielded as a political bludgeon against any and all dissenters" (*Tyranny of Clichés*, [Sentinel, 2012]: 142).

And the real problem is that it quite literally champions injustice in the name of its opposite.

∼

OVER HALF A CENTURY ago C.S. Lewis wrote a breathtaking essay called, "On the Humanitarian Theory of Justice." His concern was specifically related to criminal law and the untethering of "justice" from the concept of "punishment" or "just desserts." Instead of retribution, the humanitarian theory is concerned with "rehabilitation." Instead of talk of "punishment" we should talk with the nicer, more loving vocabulary of "therapy." Lewis pointed out that if criminal sanctions are divorced from the concept of what we actually "deserve," if we abandon, in other words, the concept of *Lex Talionis* ("Eye for an eye," arguably the most foundational legal maxim in human civilization), the result will be unimaginable tyranny. For the sanction of undergoing therapy (or "sensitivity training" or "re-education" camps) will be just as coerced as a prison sentence; only those carrying it out will be therapists and doctors doing it for "our own good," and its duration will be unknown and completely arbitrary. Paying off restitution is a pretty simple formula: getting "cured" is wholly in the eyes of the one doing the curing.

The notion of "social justice" as it is used today is simply the civil law corollary to Lewis's criminal law context. Like the "humanitarian" theory Lewis battled, we view justice as not a matter of ethics but ontology. That is, instead of viewing justice as a matter of human behavior or rectifying the consequences of wrongful actions between man and man, justice is now about rectifying states of affairs that have no perpetrator. We all know the concept of a "victimless crime." We are now obsessed with the novel concept of a "perpetratorless crime."

Think of it: we are a society of victims—victims of "structural" or "institutional" injustices, racism, so-called "micro-aggressions" (a vogue term that often seems to mean "having your feelings hurt"), bigotry, homophobia, misogyny, discrimination, poverty—but we are woefully short of actual perpetrators. Who, exactly, is responsible for these social "injustices"? What have they done? What should their sentence be? Who will impose it? We are talking about allegedly "unjust" states of affairs with no one in particular committing any actual observable injustices. When justice is conceived in other than retributive terms, it becomes an instrument of raw, arbitrary tyranny.

The reality is that there are, for lack of a better term, societal outcomes that are "natural" (as much as it is a misnomer to call a fallen world "natural.") They are simply the outworking or products of free human interactions. The economic inequities produced by a free market, for example, are the result of factors so numerous they are, for all practical purposes, infinite. Personal choices, good or bad, wise or foolish, the social status one is born into, whether educational opportunities are pursued, the presence or absence of good role models—all these things contribute to a variety of outcomes in life. Outcomes for which nobody in particular is "at fault."

Yet advocates of social justice contend that we must rectify these sorts of natural outcomes. And to do that, a perpetrator must be identified and forced to pay the necessary restitution. In the case of the "social justice" issue of poverty, the obvious culprit should be those who aren't poor. The "injustice" is ontological, a state of affairs, not ethical, the result of a person being wronged. But finding someone blameworthy in these sorts of natural societal outcomes becomes something completely arbitrary. Punishing a successful person simply because he's successful and, well, available, is a strange notion of "justice." Historically, one would call punishing somebody not guilty of a crime "injustice." But if it is done with the right motives—that is, if it supplies the remedy for social injustice—it is a matter of (as our President once put it) "basic fairness."

We ought to see that this drive for social justice is, at bottom, a theological impulse. What the advocates of social justice are really saying is that natural outcomes—that is, outcomes not produced by actual culpable human behavior—are intolerable. These outcomes must be smoothed out and made more equitable. In other words, it is not "injustice" that makes them unhappy; it is the *providence of God* with which they are unsatisfied. The sovereignty of God in their view is producing the wrong outcomes. We know better. More than that, this is an attack of the ethical goodness of God; he is either incompetent or morally perverse. Our moral sense must gain priority over his.

So the solution is what it has always been in the progressive view of things. Since Hegel modern progressivism has clearly under-stood that the State must embody the divine; the State must replace God and become its own providence, ordering all things to suit its whims.

But the State is not God. It doesn't have the goodness, the omniscience, nor the omnipotence to justly order all natural societal outcomes. And when it tries, it should not surprise us that it makes a mess of things. Idols always do a very bad job playing God. In this case the State must find someone to bear the brunt of the "restitution" necessary, and by definition this must be something arbitrary—or, to put a fine point on it, something unjust. So the rich man—or, even more in vogue, the hateful, bigoted Christian must be made to pay for the injustice and disorder hindering our egalitarian utopia, even if he or she isn't guilty of anything in particular. A Christian baker forced to attend "sensitivity training," a Christian photographer put out of business, a Christian florist who loses her livelihood, all are made the scapegoat in the literal Old Testament sense of the term. We will lay our sins on them and they must be exiled to pay for our "social injustices."

IT IS ALMOST ENOUGH to remind us of another time and place where a civil authority fancied itself divine. The Roman Empire was itself wracked with social disorder and then, as now, it was members of the Christian community that were made scapegoats. They were enemies of humanity for not acknowledging and worshiping the State as God and bowing to its efforts to effect the "common good"—efforts that involved, among other things, the eradication of "undesirables." The parallels are uncanny. We, too, have been declared enemies of humanity, no less by a sitting "Justice" of the United States Supreme Court, for not bowing to the State's whims. A reporter for the newspaper of record, *The New York Times*, says that we must be "stamped out, ruthlessly." Given that the collective memory of life under Nero still exists, we might nervously wonder what he means by "ruthlessly."

On the surface, this is all quite depressing. The word justice has been co-opted and put into service as its very opposite: the righting of every imaginable "wrong" by way of sacrifice—not blood sacrifice, yet, thankfully, but sacrifice nonetheless. And it is only going to get worse before it gets better.

But there is a silver lining, something to encourage us. Whenever an idolatrous State starts blaming Christians, specifically, for hindering its social justice aims, history indicates that we are doing something very right.

And, contrary to those who constantly claim to be on the "right side of history," history actually tells us who wins in the end. And it isn't them.

29

THE SEXUAL REVOLUTION, ENTERTAINMENT, AND CHRISTIAN ART

Opening remarks for the Center For Cultural Leadership annual symposium, held in Saratoga, California in October, 2015.

The sexual revolution was in large part successful because it used entertainment media as a principal tool of cultural subversion. There were other tools, of course: the massive takeover of academia and political activism, to name two. But when we ask the question, "What entertains you?" we are getting closer to the center of the cultural upheaval of the past five decades. We are asking a personal question at the heart of our identities: what delights you? What satisfies you? It is the question of what you—or society more broadly—worship. If you subvert and change the very nature of what entertains people, you can change the object of their worship. That means you change people, because human beings become what they worship. That means you change culture.

Many understand that the recent victories of the sexual revolution were achieved because of the contributions of the entertainment industry. Lawyers are not responsible for *Obergefell*. That distinction belongs to *Will & Grace*. No—actually, that is not true. I would argue that it is considerably more subtle than that: we owe the collapse of sexual ethics to Archie Bunker.

∽

THE YEAR WAS 1971, during the peak years of cultural turmoil. The show was *All in the Family*. What was the show about? Everybody thought it was about the Bunker family, but it wasn't. It was about *the* family. That is, the institution. And it doesn't take too much skill in hindsight to observe the message: the family as it existed up until 1971, purely typified by its leader, Archie, is an outdated, patriarchal, homophobic, narrow-minded, and bigoted institution. It's a radical message, one that never would have stood a chance if it attempted its cultural *coup d'etat* by demanding immediate acquiescence. It succeeded by making Archie... *entertaining*. The lovable, but woefully misguided, Archie Bunker. The current show *Modern Family* owes its existence to *All in the Family*.

Hollywood continued to push the boundaries further and in every direction using the same playbook. *Three's Company* soon directly attacked the outdated, prudish convictions against cohabitation—the "villain" of the show is the landlord, who only allows the newfangled "progressive" living arrangement because they trick him into thinking the male character is gay—of which he also, of course, disapproves. Fathers became optional first and famously with *Murphy Brown*, and later completely eclipsed with the *Gilmore Girls*. Homosexuality was given beautiful, airbrushed treatment in *Will & Grace*, and soon thereafter HBO's *Big Love* gave polygamy its day in the sun. *Sex and the City* glamorized the casual hookup lifestyle. Meanwhile, at the box office one "romantic comedy" after another preached the message that personal self-fulfillment exhausts the meaning of romance, marriage, and weddings. The ripple effect of these main stage attractions spilled into everything, with the eventual result being the complete normalization of rampant promiscuity. *Frasier* is (in my humble opinion) the greatest sitcom ever produced—hilarious, consistent, warm, character-driven, and brilliant in nearly every way. Yet it is difficult to miss how normal is the portrayal of Frasier's rather casual sex life. That is precisely where the architects of the sexual revolution were aiming. Their radicalism succeeded by being entertaining radicalism.

~

WHERE ARE WE NOW? We have largely lost this long, quiet, guer-rilla campaign against the family as the institutional channel for human sexuality. And we can certainly say that the sexual revolu-tion's entertainment victory has brought in its wake important political and legal victories.

There are, however, silver linings in all these dark clouds.

First, we need to remember—we must always remember—that the war against sexual purity and the family is a war against God. And that means it is a war against reality. Wars against reality cannot truly succeed. Hollywood can turn Bacchanalian promis-cuity into a virtue, but it has no cure for the ills it produces—fatherlessness, single motherhood, poverty, depression, addiction, and crime. As someone important once put it, "the wages of sin is death," and the real-world slaying is often done by sin's own effects. Just this month *Playboy* magazine announced it will no longer publish nude photographs; not because they've experienced some sudden conversion, but because the culture of pornography it created is literally destroying their business.

Second, since this is a war against reality itself, the more the bitter fruit of the sexual revolution is felt—that is, *the more successful it is*—the more likely it shapes its own demise. The Prodigal Son had an epiphany when he got to the pig trough, and I believe prodigal cultures can experience such epiphanies, too. As an exam-ple, I would point to the fact that in recent years there have been a number of films that are almost unintentionally pro-life, like *Juno* and *Knocked Up*. The recent film *Don Jon* explored the devastating effects of pornography on sexual intimacy, *Chef* is a full-throated anthem of praise for fatherhood and marriage, and one of the top rated television shows is called *Parenthood*. These are early signs of some people waking up.

Third, as far as entertainment goes, there are frankly few boundaries left to press. Unless HBO decides to produce a block-buster series glorifying bestiality—and I wouldn't put it past them—the agenda items are frankly tapped out. Who is a rebel when the revolutionaries win? Someday, hopefully soon, to be "edgy" and revolutionary in entertainment art will mean moving back toward the reality that marriage and family are beautiful, noble, and the way God intended it.

Finally—and this is more a challenge and opportunity than it is a silver lining—Christians need to be in the entertainment business. Note: I did not say, "The preaching and teaching business." That is the job description of "pastor" or "teacher," not "filmmaker." Christians have not been particularly good at film, which is a whole discussion of its own that we could take all day to discuss. But one reason is that they do not fully understand the medium. Evangelicalism is a wordy religion, and our films do altogether too much talking. We tell, instead of show. And we try to tell everything at once, for that matter. We teach, rather than entertain and delight. It may be true that aesthetics aren't everything, but they're not *nothing*. Pictures do teach, and moving pictures can teach *movingly*.

Our films also tend toward the Gnostic in their often unrealistic portrayal of what life in a sinful world is like. The "faith based" market is, for now, completely synonymous with "uplifting and inspiring," which is why its suffering is never very gritty, its heroes never disappoint you, and why you're left unsatisfied at the end. An airbrushed, gauzy, "Christiany" world is no more real than the airbrushed, gauzy world of the sexual revolutionaries. This is God's world and his story, and that story often involves horror and tragedy. Christian entertainment needs a healthy injection of a theology of the cross.

Moreover, the sexual revolution did not make one big show pushing every boundary at once; they made lots of shows, lots of angles, lots of characters, lots of stories. Yet Christians seem intent on cramming their entire worldview, complete systematic theologies, into every single product as if God is somehow dishonored if we don't say everything. You know, it is okay for a talented Christian to write a cute romantic comedy that elevates self-sacrifice above self-indulgence. A couple of centuries ago Jane Austen did it all the time.

The opportunities have never been so widely available for people to make great cinematic art, both in television and at the box office. The democratization of the technology and delivery of entertainment makes it possible for anyone with talent, vision, and modest finances to succeed. Calling our culture back to God's design for human sexuality is going to mean—it simply must mean —using the technologies of entertainment. The answer to the question, "What entertains you?" tells you what god you worship. And the truth is there is nothing more entertaining than God—have you *seen* a Hubble telescope photograph? Have you *heard* the gospel story? Have you *felt* the transforming power of grace making beauty out of ugly things and turning trash into treasure?

Those are stories worth telling, and the only thing stopping Christians from telling them is a reductionist view of what Christian art can and should be. It is a brave new entertainment world; making art that goes against the flow of the sexual revolution requires bravery. But, on the other hand, the darkness of the current backdrop makes the truth shine all the more brightly.

❀ 30 ❀

FATHER AS DEFENDER

A memory of my youth.

I had no idea I was growing up in an idyllic slice of America that would shortly disappear. We lived on a "court," a neighborhood in which a single street forms a large rectangle, with three cul-de-sacs at the corners and only one entrance and exit. We called it "The Block." At the south end was a large, well-appointed city park, and a sidewalk cut through the middle of the interior section which made it easy for kids on the north side to cut through to the park without walking all the way around.

"Idyllic," I say, because even though these were the days of putting missing children on milk cartons, very few people were concerned about child abduction. Yes, Mrs. Harper always kept close watch on her kids—they were notoriously not allowed to "leave the block." Not even a toe could touch outside the confines of our haven. But mostly, parents just let their kids run free, especially in the summertime. We'd have late-night games of "war" with all the neighborhood kids, and the entire neighborhood was the field of play. Sporting full combat gear (purchased from the Army/Navy store), you could jump any fence or cut through any backyard without incident. Even the dogs knew every kid on the block.

In the cul-de-sac to the west of our house lived a family that was different from the rest of the block's upwardly mobile lower-middle class. I always avoided going near their house. Not because Boo Radley lived there, but something much more terrifying. Mr. Simon was a hulk of a man. He sported a thick black beard, had long hair covered by bandanas, and was never seen without his signature biker gang leathers. I have no idea what he did for a living, but whenever he was home he seemed to have only one occupation: tinkering in his garage with some kind of classic car that no matter how long he worked on it never seemed any more "restored." He chain smoked, which, while I do not recall my parents ever saying anything about it, gave a whiff of scandal to a budding Pharisee like me. If my friend Todd and I were hanging out in my front yard, we'd scurry to hide every time we heard that Harley Davidson fire up down the street. We were petrified of the man.

The Simon children (I recall two boys, and later, a younger sister) were of the annoying sort. They did not fit in with the rest of the neighborhood gang. I do not recall for certain their names, but the younger son—let's call him Jake—is the relevant subject. One fine summer day the gang (Which we called the "A-Team," after the television show dominating the airwaves at the time) was hanging out on the Harper's driveway. My two older brothers, Jeff and Dan, the Harper boys Troy and Todd, Jay Whittington, and me. I could not have been more than seven or eight years old. Also among our group was a cranky, cocky, arrogant kid of very lower-class, myste- rious parentage named—I kid you not—Rogue.

We were doing the typical "What should we do today?" mulling about when we heard Jake Simon riding down the street on his tricycle. We heard him because his ride had a very squeaky wheel. *Squeaksqueaksqueaksqueaksqueak!* When he got to the front of the driveway, he made a left turn and rode right up to the group.

"Whatchya doin?"

Rogue stepped forward, puffed out his chest and replied, "Nothing. And if you run over my foot I'll punch you."

Jake immediately put the pedal to the metal and ran over Rogue's foot. (Did I mention annoying?)

Smack!

I remember the sound like it was yesterday because it was the first time I'd ever heard that sound outside of the volume-enhanced versions in the movies. It was even *louder* than the movies. Rogue right-hooked Jake squarely in the eye. Jake fled, bawling and squeaking his way back down the street. We were all appalled, and in pathetically meek, weak, and mumbling fashion said things like, "Rogue, you really shouldn't have done that!"

Now, I don't know what got into Jake, but an hour or so later we heard that same familiar *Squeaksqueaksqueaksqueaksqueak!* He was getting back on the horse after getting bucked, I guess. Or bravely facing down his bully. Or he had just gone insane. Because, after riding back up the driveway, this time with one very puffy black eye, the conversation went exactly like this.

"Whatchya doin?"

"If you run over my foot I'll punch you."

[...]

Smack!

Directly in the *other* eye.

Bellowing wails and lamentations once again echoed and resounded over the entire block as he squeaked his way back home. The A-Team was on edge the rest of the day. Our Commander, my oldest brother Jeff, instructed everyone to lay low. We all knew trouble was brewing. It was all particularly humiliating because the A-Team, despite how it sounds just now, was a pretty welcoming gang. We were not mean. We were not bullies. We fostered *esprit de corps* and brotherhood and discipline. (Seriously, we did military drills in our backyard, in preparation for the inevitable Russian invasion.) We just happened to have a really bad seed at that moment in time, a character with a very appropriate name: there is no doubt in our minds he was "rogue."

The afternoon drifted late. We decided to cut through the block and head for the park. As we made our way up the grassy hill to the playground, I heard another thing I had never heard outside of movies: squealing tires. I jerked my head around and saw a car rounding the corner *sideways*. The engine roared and the blacktop was indelibly marred with hot rubber.

Mr. Simon was gunning for us.

We all stood, paralyzed, and watched in awe as his car careened into the parking area to an abrupt halt. He leaped out of the car, screaming at the top of his lungs. He loped to the top of the hill, towered over us, and gave us a piece of his mind. It was all such a blur I cannot remember the soliloquy. I'm pretty sure it was profanity-laced. There were dark threats. Not the "I'm going to tell your parents" kind, either. The "I'll bury you alive if you ever touch my children again" kind. He openly shamed my older brothers. That I recall. For Mr. Simon, they bore responsibility: the more powerful must protect the weak.

It was literally the first (and last) time I ever heard Mr. Simon speak. And the impression—if not the actual words—was unforgettable.

Nobody ever dared harass the Simon children again. Ever.

~

I FAINTLY RECALL NOW something odd. Mr. Simon was a very scary guy we reasonably thought was in a biker gang. He was by definition something of a misfit, especially for our neighborhood. But I now remember one of the things that made his children so annoying: they rarely uttered a sentence without the words, "*My* Dad." Nobody could ever top them in the childish game of "My Dad is better than your Dad." I was terrified of him, but they worshiped the ground he walked on. They admired him. And they loved him.

And, as everyone (the A-Team and his own children alike) discovered that day, he loved them, too. Whatever his social deficiencies, he was their lodestar, their hero, and their defender. Tire marks were laid down as testament for years.

My brother Jeff flourished into an exceptional leader. He had a highly unusual interest in the weak. He was popular in high school, part of the cool crowd, but it was his befriending and mentoring of shy, nervous freshmen that made him Captain of the cross country team. This, when he couldn't even run fast enough to obtain a varsity letter. He always had an eye for misfits and wallflowers, always bending over backward to make people welcome. It was this kind of leadership—servant leadership—that awarded him an eventual appointment to West Point and his subsequent service in Bosnia and Kosovo.

Dan, too, became a man of service to others, earning a full-ride ROTC scholarship to pursue a nursing degree. As a nurse anesthetist, he served two tours in Baghdad during the most gruesome and violent period of the war. He, too, had an eye for serving the weak and wounded in unusual ways. Once, Secretary of Defense Donald Rumsfeld stood muttering under his breath near the bed of a terribly wounded soldier. Dan intervened, saying, "Sir, he can hear you. Please talk to him." The Secretary and that soldier shared a quiet moment of powerful intimacy they will likely never forget.

FATHERHOOD IS NOT AN ABSTRACTION. That day the A-Team saw it in its raw, untamed, flesh-and-blood reality. As unlikely as it seemed to us, that "unlovable" man's children had something utterly irreplaceable: the love of a Father, protector, and defender.

And it made us all better men.

31

CHESS & TRUE FREEDOM

The game of chess is never going to rival soccer or the NFL for popularity. Five hours of watching two players sitting in chairs thinking deep thoughts doesn't seem like much widespread viewing potential. It is remarkable, then, that this month chess is enjoying global enthusiasm and popularity like it hasn't since Garry Kasparov played IBM's computer "Deep Blue" in the 1990s or, even further back, the electrifying performance of Bobby Fischer against Boris Spassky in Reykjavik, 1972.

If you're an average American, you probably don't know anything about any of it, so I want to take the opportunity to share this with you: the greatest chess player in the world is a 22-year-old Norwegian by the name of Magnus Carlsen. Get used to it, because it will likely be true for just about the remainder of your lifetime. "Greatest in the world" is not a matter of opinion, either. Carlsen possesses the highest chess rating of any player in history (2870) and is known, for the time being, as "World Number 1." Added to the mystique of youth and brilliance is the fact that Magnus is not your average awkward "chess nerd," but is athletic, affable, humble, and handsome enough to get endorsement contracts.

He is currently the challenger in a twelve game match with

reigning five-time World Champion Viswanathan Anand in Chennai, India, where he has a virtually insurmountable lead. In fact, the match may well be over as you're reading this, in a mere ten games because Magnus appears to not need the full twelve to defeat the World Champion.

I have never *watched* chess until this event. Who would? But the hype surrounding Carlsen proved too much for me to ignore, so I've been joining in with the *hundreds of millions* of others around the globe tuning in to the livestream. It has been incredibly stimulating, as the commentators do an excellent job explaining all the various scenarios that could play out with certain moves. I am too poor a player to do much guessing about the moves Grandmasters (actually, they're called "Super GMs") might make, so I think about other things.

Like how chess teaches us a fundamental lesson for life.

∼

CONTEMPORARY CULTURE TEACHES us that freedom is the ability to do whatever we desire, whenever we desire it. Creativity and fulfillment is found in a realm absent of boundaries, borders, and restraints.

But consider the following:

Chess has a finite number of pieces (32).

Chess has a finite number of squares (64).

Chess has ironclad rules of movement for every piece.

Yet the possible game variations are, for all practical purposes, *infinite*. (The actual number is 10 to the power of 120, which, sources tell me—I have no way of personally verifying it—is more than the number of atoms in the observable universe.)

You see, there are reasons people like Fischer and Spassky, Kasparov and Karpov, Carlsen and Anand dedicated and continue to dedicate their lives to understanding and playing this deeply mysterious game. Far from feeling constricted and having their style cramped by all these "squares" and "boundaries" and "rules," they instead find virtually infinite *creativity* and *freedom*. They simply wouldn't—and couldn't—if it were otherwise. The strict rules do not result in boring, uniform results, but rather endless possibilities and new ideas. Sometimes they result in games of jaw-dropping brilliance.

Those 32 pieces and 64 squares teach us that true freedom, creativity, and fulfillment only occur in the context of order. That means boundaries and rules.

So it is with this morally ordered universe. Personal freedom, creativity, and fulfillment are not found in doing whatever you want, whenever you want, however you want, with or to whomever you want. They are found when you conform to the moral order of things. Sometimes you might not see it right away. Many a chess game has a long, painful "middle game" when you have to slog it out for twenty moves before the end is clearly seen. Who cannot relate to that as an analogy for much of life?

For example, it relates to economics: cheap, ill-gotten gain isn't fulfilling, but an honest dollar (earned success) is. Or how about sex? Which is more fulfilling: sticking with marriage vows over the long term, even in rough times, or being tossed to and fro by every fleeting wind of desire?

Whatever you happen to be struggling with, whether it is hating that certain somebody (anger), cheating on that upcoming test (lying), or maybe over-leveraging yourself with debt (greed and coveting), remember this simple lesson from the game of chess: the rules do not hamper your freedom.

They make you truly free.

32

JANE AUSTEN, PERSPECTIVALISM,
AND THE THINKING MAN

I have a confession to make. Not the sort of confession one needs to feel ashamed of, but the kind of confession that simply lets others in on a little-known fact. In my briefcase I have one of those interior slots that is designed for things like laptop computer cables and that sort of thing. This little pocket is the perfect size for another possession of mine: my beautiful little cloth-bound edition of Jane Austen's *Emma*. Whenever I find myself with spare moments, most recently while taking a lunch break fishing on the Stillwater River, I pull out that little red volume and read it. I find myself amazed time and again at the profound insights I find.

Jane Austen was not a philosopher. She was the daughter of a country minister. She never traveled far, which is why her books always display the kind of life she knew: small, English country communities. In her books, the big metropolis of London usually seems some far-distant place. But this lack of broader exposure didn't harm her ability to penetrate into the inner sanctum of the human heart in the slightest. In my estimation, *Emma* is one of the finest novels ever written. It is not just a wonderful read, but a very profound piece of philosophy.

Our postmodern age in its typical hubris likes to think that we are the first to understand the "situatedness" of human knowledge, that nobody has a "birds-eye," objective view of things. We are the first to break free from the shackles, we are told, of the "totalizing" visions of the Enlightenment and realize the epistemic limitations of the human condition. Yet here a humble, provincial woman in the late 18th century writes a novel that has as its principal subject all of these very issues. In fact, she puts on a veritable epistemological clinic.

Emma Woodhouse is utterly self-deceived. She thinks—nay, she is convinced—that she has everything figured out. Austen brilliantly places the reader inside Emma's skin; what Emma thinks she knows, the reader thinks he or she knows. Emma's omniscience and self-certainty is the reader's omniscience and self-certainty. Then Austen slowly chips away at Emma's supposedly "objective" perspective on things to reveal complete and total self-deception. She is blinded by self-reinforcing presuppositions and preconceptions.

There is much more to the book than this, of course. One could also view it as an extended commentary on the Proverbs 27:6: "Wounds from a friend can be trusted, but an enemy multiplies kisses." For there is only one person in the book who loves Emma enough to tell her the truth about herself, and only in heeding these admonitions is happiness to be found.

But recently Chapter 18 deeply impressed me. It begins: "Mr. Frank Churchill did not come." The entirety of the chapter is a simple conversation between Emma and Mr. Knightley about the reasons for Mr. Churchill's absence from the Village of Highbury, and, more importantly, what conclusions one can and should draw about his character by his absence. For, surely, Mr. Churchill's presence in Highbury is required. On that everyone is agreed. You see, as a young boy Frank went to live with his Aunt after his mother's death. His father has recently remarried, and the now-young man has yet to visit to pay his respects to his new stepmother. In fact, he has promised to come many times, only to be detained at the last moment. These are not the actions of a proper gentleman.

Emma is extremely generous in her attitude, believing that the reason for his absence can be attributed solely to Frank's loathsome Aunt, and not to some defect in his character. Mr. Knightley, on the other hand, lays the bulk of the blame directly on Frank: "The Churchills are very likely in fault. But I dare say he might come if he would."

What follows is a deeply informed, philosophically fascinating conversation about ethics, involving not merely the "Norm" of ethics (what should be done), but also the "Situation" involved (extenuating circumstances) and the person performing the action, or the "Existential" perspective. Mr. Knightley is hung up on just the Norm: if the young man should come, he ought simply to come. If he fails, this reveals a serious character defect:

> If Frank Churchill had wanted to see his father, he would have contrived it between September and January. A man at his age—what is he?—three or four-and-twenty cannot be without the means of doing as much as that. It is impossible.

Emma, on the other hand, cannot get away from the Situational perspective: Frank's attachments and duties to his Aunt preclude his duty to his stepmother. Viewed in this light, it is not a character flaw, but to his credit that he performs his duty to his Aunt, the woman who raised him. She says, "It is very unfair to judge of anybody's conduct without an intimate knowledge of their situation." Both perspectives, the Normative and the Situational, affect what one concludes about the Existential: the character of Frank Churchill himself.

So profound is this little tri-perspectival ethical conversation that when Mr. Knightley emphatically insists that if he were to be in Frank's position, he would tell off his Aunt and come to High-

bury straight away, whatever the consequences, Emma responds
with this deft counter:

 I can imagine that if you, as you are, Mr. Knightley,
were to be transported and placed all at once in Mr.
Frank Churchill's situation, you would be able to say
and do just what you have been recommending for
him; and it might have a very good effect. The
Churchills might not have a word to say in return; but
then, you would have no habits of early obedience and
long observance to break through. To him who has, it
might not be so easy to burst forth at once into
perfect independence, and set all their claims on his
gratitude and regard at naught. He may have as strong
a sense of what would be right, as you can have,
without being so equal under particular circumstances
to act up to it.

So much for postmodernity being the first age to recognize the
situational and existential character of ethics! Yes, Mr. Knightley
could perform his recommended course of action; it is a different
question altogether whether Frank Churchill, being the person he
is, the upbringing he had, the familial habits he formed, could do
likewise. Emma argues that Mr. Knightley's hyper-normative
reading of things is a pure abstraction, divorced from reality.

Now this, of course, is pure irony on Ms. Austen's part, for
Emma Woodhouse is the worst person in the world to be giving
advice on refraining from preconceived notions and fully seeking to
understand people and their situations in life. In fact, this passage
comes just after Emma has just so profoundly failed to understand
the character and situation of a certain Mr. Elton!

Oh, there is much to mine, and I suppose I'll have my little red
book (way better than Mao's) in my briefcase pocket for years to
come. When I want a great story, great characters, and great food

for reflection and thought, I can always rely on Miss Austen. She writes books for thinking men.

❧ 33 ☙

A NOTE ON HARRY POTTER

W hat more is there to be said about Harry Potter? Since its explosive entrance into the public marketplace, Christians have debated *ad nauseam* the relative merits and demerits of J.K. Rowling's seven-part masterpiece. Everything that can be said about the legitimacy of Christian enjoyment of Rowling's world filled with "witchcraft and wizardry" has been said, many, many times. Or has it?

I've done my share of reading these debates, and, believe it or not, I think there is more to be said. This is fresh on my mind because of a fine evening I enjoyed last night on my back porch talking it over with my sister. And we agree that there is one crucial, and yet obvious, aspect of all this that has not been noticed by any of the participants of the debate.

Let me just say this first: I believe that Christians are absolutely right to view (at least initially) the series with suspicion and skepticism. That is because on the very surface of it, Rowling uses the categories of, well, "witchcraft and wizardry." These are loaded terms, and the Bible is very clear that these types of occult practices are deadly, dangerous, and forbidden. I don't hold in contempt anyone who in good conscience avoids this literature on that basis alone. I am somewhat more skeptical, however, of the many Christians who deplore Rowling but just *l-o-v-e* Tolkien and Lewis. A bit of consistency would be nice.

One recent author has a whole chapter in a book devoted to showing how the "magic" of Lewis and Tolkien is good, but the "magic" in Rowling is bad. Now, that's not a bad thing to set out to show. But avoiding being a complete embarrassment in the process would be helpful. He baldly claims that in Rowling's books, witches and wizards are viewed as the "good guys," and the "Muggles," people without magical powers, are viewed as the "bad guys." No, I am not making this up. Clearly, for anybody who has read the books, it is obvious that this gentleman has never even come close to reading the books. (Hint: the only people in the books who hold that view are the *bad* guys. The good guys are dedicated to rejecting that view.)

Having read the books through twice, and the Deathly Hallows three times, I think all efforts to paint Rowling's magical world as "bad," while retaining Lewis's and Tolkien's worlds as "good" is a doomed enterprise. And here's why:

There is a fundamental feature of Rowling's world that forms the backbone of the story and which Christian critics have not appreciated:

Non-magical people (Muggles) cannot—*cannot*—obtain magical powers.

I'll say that again:

Non-magical people (Muggles) cannot—*cannot*—obtain magical powers.

This means that the magic in Rowling's world is not "occult" magic. Occultism is the idea that there is a power that can be "tapped into," and people are overcome by the lust for this power, seeking to gain control of it and to manipulate it for their own ends. This is what causes the concern in Christian circles: that Rowling's books will tempt young people to experiment in the occult. But any good reader of the books knows that if you are a Muggle, as all readers are, this realm is simply unavailable to you. In the nature of the case, in Rowling's world, Muggles simply have no access to magical powers. By definition. There is nothing to "tap into." You are either born subject to the magical world or you are not. There is no transfer from one realm to the next.

This should lead us to consider how "unspiritual" the magic is in Rowling's world. Magical power is subject to laws. There are *rules*, as Hermione Granger is constantly reminding her friends. You cannot conjure something out of nothing, for example. This is why young witches and wizards go to *school*. The books center, after all, around Hogwarts School for Witchcraft and Wizardry. Young ones must become educated as to the laws that govern the unique world to which they belong.

In a word: the "magic" in Rowling's books is another, separate, natural law.

Harry Potter's world is divided between two realms of natural law: the ordinary and the magical. And here's the most important part: both realms are subject to a higher moral realm, with love of others being the highest law. This is not occultism. Young witches and wizards in the books are simply subject to the magical realm in which they find themselves, and they must learn and obey the "rules" of magic, and submit themselves to the ethics of love.

Oh, but somebody might say, there *is* "dark magic" in the books. Well, of course, Tom Riddle becomes an expert in "dark magic." This is magic that is the antithesis to the ethics of love and self-sacrifice, magic done for pure, autonomous, murderous ends. So, magical natural law can be abused for "dark" ends. This proves that this is "occultism," right?

Not so fast. Let's come back to reality for a moment. We believe in natural law. The world is ordered by natural (e.g., biological, physical) principles. We believe in "science," not "magic." If what I am saying about Rowling's magical world being one of "natural law" is right (and I believe it is), then it would follow that there would have to be, even theoretically, something like "dark science," right? That would be how the analogy would have to work. Surely such an idea is ludicrous, right?

But there is such a thing as "dark science." It is called cloning human embryos for experimentation that might allow us to, like Voldemort, live forever. It is called manipulating ("enriching") uranium to kill hundreds of thousands of people. It is called manipulating diseases for use in biological weapons. And so on. There are plenty of Tom Riddles in our own world. No, they don't wear black wizarding robes. They wear white lab coats.

Rowling's wizarding world is, therefore, an analogue of the natural world. Just as there is "good" magic, magic that operates as designed and subject to the highest ethical law of love, there is also "good" science, science that operates as designed and subject to the highest ethical law of love. Just as there is "dark" magic, magic that resists the ethic of love, so there is "dark" science, science that resists the ethic of love.

The way Rowling has set this up makes it, in my estimation, decidedly not "occult." The magical world is not a free-for-all of demonic powers to be manipulated, but a realm of rules and laws and ethical imperatives. And it is not a realm that can be "tapped" into in any way.

One might not like the Harry Potter saga for other reasons (though I cannot imagine what they might be.) But I don't think you can get rid of Hogwarts on the basis of "magic" and get to keep Narnia and Middle Earth at the same time. After all, the climax of Lewis's *Prince Caspian* is a full-scale séance!

I will close by noting that countless "spin-off" works, those juvenile fiction authors seeking to cash in on Rowling's success, very probably do not have a magical world as well-defined as hers. In my own admittedly casual perusal of juvenile fiction shelves, there is an awful lot of clearly and truly "occult" books for young people to read.

It is just that J.K. Rowling's are not among them.

❧ 34 ❧

SYMPATHY FOR THE DEVIL

After attending the film Noah *on its opening weekend, I published this review late on a Sunday night. By mid-week it was viral, and I was suddenly being interviewed on national radio. All told, the review was read by over a million people. Coincidentally—who can say?—the film collapsed at the box office the following weekend.*

In Darren Aronofsky's new star-gilt silver screen epic, *Noah*, Adam and Eve are luminescent and fleshless, right up until the moment they eat the forbidden fruit.

Such a notion isn't found in the Bible, of course. This, among the multitude of Aronofsky's other imaginative details like giant Lava Monsters, has caused many a reviewer's head to be scratched. Conservative-minded evangelicals write off the film because of the "liberties" taken with the text of Genesis, while a more liberal-minded group stands in favor of cutting the director some slack. After all, we shouldn't expect a professed atheist to have the same ideas of "respecting" sacred texts the way a Bible-believer would.

Both groups have missed the mark entirely. Aronofsky hasn't "taken liberties" with anything.

The Bible is not his text.

In his defense, I suppose, the film wasn't advertised as such. Nowhere is it said that this movie is an adaptation of Genesis. It was never advertised as *"The Bible's Noah,"* or *"The Biblical Story of Noah."* In our day and age we are so living in the leftover atmosphere of Christendom that when somebody says they want to do "Noah," everybody *assumes* they mean a rendition of the *Bible* story. That isn't what Aronofsky had in mind at all. I'm sure he was only too happy to let his studio go right on assuming that, since if they knew what he was really up to they never would have allowed him to make the movie.

LET'S go back to our luminescent first parents. I recognized the motif instantly as one common to the ancient religion of Gnosticism. Here's a 2nd century A.D. description about what a sect called the Ophites believed:

> Adam and Eve formerly had light, luminous, and so to speak spiritual bodies, as they had been fashioned. But when they came here, the bodies became dark, fat, and idle. –Irenaeus of Lyon, *Against Heresies*, I, 30.9

It occurred to me that a mystical tradition more closely related to Judaism, called *Kabbalah* (which the singer Madonna made popular a decade ago or so), surely would have held a similar view, since it is essentially a form of *Jewish* Gnosticism. I dusted off (No, really: I had to dust it) my copy of Adolphe Franck's 19th century work, *The Kabbalah*, and quickly confirmed my suspicions:

> Before they were beguiled by the subtleness of the serpent, Adam and Eve were not only exempt from the need of a body, but did not even have a body— that is to say, they were not of the earth.

Franck quotes from the *Zohar,* one of *Kabbalah's* sacred texts:

> When our forefather Adam inhabited the Garden of Eden, he was clothed, as all are in heaven, with a garment made of the higher light. When he was driven from the Garden of Eden and was compelled to submit to the needs of this world, what happened? God, the Scriptures tell us, made Adam and his wife tunics of skin and clothed them; for before this they had tunics of light, of that higher light used in Eden [...]

Obscure stuff, I know. But curiosity overtook me and I dove right down the rabbit hole.

I discovered what Darren Aronofsky's first feature film was: *Pi.* Want to know its subject matter? Do you? Are you sure?

Kabbalah.

If you think that's a coincidence, you may want a loved one to schedule you a brain scan.

Have I got your attention? Good.

～

THE WORLD of Aronofsky's *Noah* is a thoroughly Gnostic one: a graded universe of "higher" and "lower." The "spiritual" is good, and way, way, way "up there" where the ineffable, *unspeaking* god dwells, and the "material" is bad, and way, way down here where our spirits are encased in material flesh. This is not only true of the fallen sons and daughters of Adam and Eve, but of fallen angels, who are explicitly depicted as being spirits *trapped* inside a material "body" of cooled molten lava.

Admittedly, they make pretty nifty movie characters, but they're also notorious in Gnostic speculation. Gnostics call them *Archons,* lesser divine beings or angels who aid "The Creator" in forming the visible universe. And *Kabbalah* has a pantheon of angelic beings of its own all up and down the ladder of "divine being." And fallen angels are never totally fallen in this brand of mysticism. To quote the *Zohar* again, a central *Kabbalah* text: "All things of which this world consists, the spirit as well as the body, will return to the principle and the root from which they came." Funny. That's exactly what happens to Aronofsky's Lava Monsters. They redeem themselves, shed their outer material skin, and fly back to the heavens. Incidentally, I noticed that in the film, as the family is traveling through a desolate wasteland, Shem asks his father: "Is this a *Zohar* mine?" Yep. That's the name of *Kabbalah's* sacred text.

The entire movie is, figuratively, a "Zohar" mine.

If there was any doubt about these "Watchers," Aronofsky gives several of them names: Semyaza, Magog, and Rameel. They're all well-known demons in the Jewish mystical tradition, not only in *Kabbalah* but also in the book of *1 Enoch*.

What!? *Demons* are redeemed? Adolphe Franck explains the cosmology of *Kabbalah*:

> Nothing is absolutely bad; nothing is accursed forever —not even the archangel of evil or the venomous beast, as he is sometimes called. There will come a time when he will recover his name and his angelic nature.

Okay. That's weird. But, hey, everybody in the film seems to worship "The Creator," right? Surely it's got that in its favor!

Except that when Gnostics speak about "The Creator" they are *not talking about God.* Oh, here in an affluent world living off the fruits of Christendom the term "Creator" generally denotes the true and living God. But here's a little "Gnosticism 101" for you: the *Creator of the material world* is an ignorant, arrogant, jealous, exclusive, violent, low-level, bastard son of a low level deity. He's responsible for creating the "unspiritual" world of flesh and matter, and he himself is so ignorant of the spiritual world he fancies himself the "only God" and demands absolute obedience. They generally call him "Yahweh." Or other names, too (Ialdabaoth, for example).

This Creator tries to keep Adam and Eve from the true knowledge of the divine and, when they disobey, flies into a rage and boots them from the garden.

In other words, in case you're losing the plot here: *The serpent was right all along.* This "god," "The Creator," whom they are worshiping is *withholding* something from them that the serpent will provide: divinity itself.

The world of Gnostic mysticism is bewildering with a myriad of varieties. But, generally speaking, they hold in common that the serpent is "Sophia," "Mother," or "Wisdom." The serpent represents the *true* divine, and the claims of "The Creator" are false.

So is the serpent a major character in the film?

Let's go back to the movie. The action opens when Lamech is about to bless his son, Noah. Lamech, rather strangely for a patriarch of a family that follows God, takes out a sacred relic, *the skin of the serpent from the Garden of Eden.* He wraps it around his arm, stretches out his hand to touch his son—except, just then, a band of marauders interrupts them and the ceremony isn't completed. Lamech gets killed, and the "villain" of the film, Tubal-Cain, steals the snakeskin. Noah, in other words, doesn't get whatever benefit the serpent's skin was to bestow.

The skin doesn't light up magically on Tubal-Cain's arm, so apparently he doesn't get "enlightened," either. And that's why everybody in the film, including protagonist and antagonist, Noah and Tubal-Cain, is worshiping "The Creator." *They are all deluded.* Let me clear something up here: lots of reviewers expressed some bewilderment over the fact there aren't any likable characters and that they *all* seem to be worshiping the same God. Tubal-Cain and his clan are wicked and evil and, as it turns out, Noah's pretty bad himself when he abandons Ham's girlfriend and almost slays two newborn children. Some thought this was some kind of profound commentary on how there's evil in all of us. Here's an excerpt from the *Zohar*, the sacred text of *Kabbalah*:

> Two beings [Adam and Nachash—the Serpent] had intercourse with Eve [the Second woman], and she conceived from both and bore two children. Each followed one of the male parents, and their spirits parted, one to this side and one to the other, and similarly their characters. On the side of Cain are all the haunts of the evil species; from the side of Abel comes a more merciful class, yet not wholly beneficial —good wine mixed with bad.

Sound familiar? Yes. Darren Aronofsky's *Noah*, to the "T."

Anyway, everybody is worshiping the *evil* deity. Who wants to destroy *everybody*. (By the way, in *Kabbalah* many worlds have already been created and destroyed.) Both Tubal-Cain *and* Noah have identical scenes, looking into the heavens and asking, "Why won't you *speak to me?*" "The Creator" has abandoned them all because he intends to kill them all.

Noah had been given a vision of the coming deluge. He's drowning, but sees animals floating to the surface to the safety of the ark. No indication whatsoever is given that Noah is to be saved; Noah conspicuously makes that part up during an awkward moment explaining things to his family. He is sinking while the animals, "the innocent," are rising. "The Creator" who gives Noah his vision wants *all the humans dead*.

Many reviewers thought Noah's change into a homicidal maniac on the ark, wanting to kill his son's two newborn daughters, was a weird plot twist. It isn't weird at all. In the Director's view, Noah is worshiping a *false, homicidal maniac* of a god. The more faithful and "godly" Noah becomes, the more *homicidal* he becomes. He is becoming every bit the "image of god" that the "evil" guy who keeps talking about the "image of god," Tubal-Cain, is.

But Noah fails "The Creator." He cannot wipe out all life like his god wants him to do. "When I looked at those two girls, my heart was filled with nothing but *love*," he says. Noah now has something "The Creator" doesn't. Love. And Mercy. But where did he get it? And why now?

In the immediately preceding scene Noah killed Tubal-Cain and *recovered the snakeskin relic*: "Sophia," "Wisdom," the true light of the divine. Just a coincidence, I'm sure.

Okay, I'm almost done. The rainbows don't come at the end because God makes a covenant with Noah. The rainbows appear when Noah sobers up and *embraces the serpent*. He wraps the skin around his arm, and blesses his family. It is not *God* that commissions them to now multiply and fill the earth, but Noah, in the first person, "I," wearing the serpent talisman. (Oh, and by the way, it's not accidental that the rainbows are all *circular*. The circle of the "One," the *Ein Sof*, in *Kabbalah*, is the sign of monism.)

Notice this thematic change: Noah was in a drunken stupor the scene before. Now he is sober and "enlightened." Filmmakers *never* do that by accident.

He's transcended and outgrown that homicidal, jealous deity.

Let me issue a couple of caveats to all this: Gnostic speculation is a diverse thing. Some groups appear *radically* "dualist," where "The Creator" really is a different "god" altogether. Others are more "monist," where God exists in a series of descending emanations. Others have it that the lower deity grows and matures and himself ascends the "ladder" or "chain" of being to higher heights. *Noah* probably fits a little in each category. It's hard to tell.

My other caveat is this: there is no doubt a *ton* of *Kabbalist* imagery, quotations, and themes in this movie that I couldn't pick up in a single sitting. For example, since *Kabbalah* takes its flights of fancy generally based on Hebrew letters and numbers, I did notice that the "Watchers" appeared to be deliberately shaped like Hebrew letters. But you could not pay me to go see this movie again so I could further drill into the *Zohar* mine to see what I could find. On a purely cinematic viewpoint, I found most of it unbearably boring.

What I can say on one viewing is this:

Darren Aronofsky has produced a retelling of the Noah story

without reference to the Bible at all. This was not, as he claimed, just a storied tradition of run-of-the-mill Jewish "Midrash." This was a thoroughly pagan retelling of the Noah story direct from Kabbalist and Gnostic sources. To my mind, there is simply no doubt about this.

So let me tell you what the real scandal in all of this is.

It isn't that he made a film that departed from the biblical story. It isn't that disappointed and overheated Christian critics had expectations set too high.

The scandal is this: of all the Christian leaders who went to great lengths to endorse this movie (for whatever reasons: "it's a conversation starter," "at least Hollywood is doing something on the Bible," etc.), and all of the Christian leaders who panned it for "not following the Bible"...

Not one of them could identify a blatantly Gnostic subversion of the biblical story when it was right in front of their faces.

I believe Aronofsky did it as an experiment to make fools of us: "You are so ignorant that I can put Noah (granted, it's *Russell Crowe!*) up on the big screen and portray him literally as the 'seed of the Serpent' and you all will watch my studio's screening and endorse it."

He's having quite the laugh. And shame on everyone who bought it.

And *what a Gnostic experiment*! In Gnosticism, only the "elite" are "in the know" and have the secret knowledge. Everybody else are dupes and ignorant fools. The "event" of this movie is intended to illustrate the Gnostic premise. We are dupes and fools. Would Christendom awake, please?

In response, I have one simple suggestion:

Henceforth, not a single seminary degree is granted unless the student demonstrates that he has read, digested, and understood Irenaeus of Lyon's *Against Heresies*.

Because it's the 2nd century all over again.

❧ 35 ❧

GOD OF SIGNS & WONDERS

roken relationships sometimes seem absolutely hopeless.
Beyond repair. Sometimes the intractability of conflict
moves us to despair. There seems no way forward. The
trenches are dug. Nobody is going to budge. One might just as soon
raise a person from the dead as achieve reconciliation with a bitter
enemy.

And that is why, to me, reconciliation is proof that God exists.
The God who really did raise Jesus from the dead (and thereby
achieved reconciliation with us, his enemies) continues to exercise
that resurrection power in the world, achieving what should rightly
be called "signs and wonders." Signs and wonders, you say? Surely
hyperbole, right?

Not really. Bear with me. Today I celebrate one such miracle, in
honor and remembrance of the life and work of Dr. Martin Luther
King, Jr. Today is, of course, the day set aside to celebrate Dr.
King's legacy, and I recommend that you do that by watching his "I
Have a Dream" speech. Without fail, it brings tears to my eyes:

I have a dream that one day my four little children will live in a land where they are judged not by the color of their skin, but by the content of their character.

Truly legendary rhetoric, and we should actively work to preserve it in our collective American memory. I recommend following that up by reading Dr. King's "Letter From a Birmingham Jail," a tract which, to my mind, belongs in the canon of great American political writings. Who can read this and remain unmoved?

 I guess it is easy for those who have never felt the stinging darts of segregation to say 'wait.' But when you have seen vicious mobs lynch your mothers and fathers at will and drown your sisters and brothers at whim; when you have seen hate-filled policemen curse, kick, brutalize, and even kill your black brothers and sisters with impunity; when you see the vast majority of your twenty million Negro brothers smothering in an airtight cage of poverty in the midst of an affluent society; when you suddenly find your tongue twisted and your speech stammering as you seek to explain to your six-year-old daughter why she cannot go to the public amusement park that has just been advertised on television, and see tears welling up in her little eyes when she is told that Funtown is closed to colored children, and see the depressing clouds of inferiority begin to form in her little mental sky, and see her begin to distort her little personality by unconsciously developing a bitterness toward white people; when you have to concoct an answer for a five-year-old son asking in agonizing pathos, "Daddy, why do white people treat colored people so mean?"; when you take a cross-country drive and find it necessary to sleep night after night in the uncomfortable corners of your automobile because no motel will accept you; when you are humiliated day in and day out by nagging signs reading "white" and "colored"; when your first name becomes "nigger" and your middle name becomes "boy" (however old you are) and your last name becomes "John," and when your wife and mother are never given the respected title "Mrs."; when you are harried by day and haunted by night by the fact that you are a Negro, living constantly at tiptoe stance, never knowing what to expect next, and plagued with inner fears and outer resentments; when you are forever fighting a degenerating sense of "nobodyness"—then you will understand why we find it difficult to wait. There comes a time when the cup of endurance runs over and men are no longer willing to be plunged into an abyss of injustice where they experience the bleakness of corroding despair. I hope, sirs, you can understand our legitimate and unavoidable impatience.

BACK TO THE "I HAVE A DREAM" speech. Dr. King began by invoking the name of Lincoln, under whose symbolic statue he stood when giving the speech in 1963. He was bringing to mind, of course, the great conflict of the civil war. And he effectively went on to describe the gaping chasm between the great promise of emancipation and the reality on the ground a hundred years later.

One of the evidences of just how extravagantly gracious God has been to the American people is the fact that we forget just how deep the divisions over race once were. No, we don't "forget." We have *no concept whatsoever just how dire the situation was*. The situation at the close of the war was utterly hopeless. Beyond repair. The breach between North and South would never be healed. The breach between white and black would never be healed. This is not hyperbole.

On April 1, 1865 the Richmond Times-Dispatch opined: "After what has occurred for four long years, the future unity of America is a dream of maniacs." That's right: only a "maniac" could dream of a United States. In the editor's opinion, "the mode of conducting this war had been shaped for no other purpose than to render a restoration of the old Union impossible." He is referring, of course, to the brutality of Sherman's campaign in the South:

> Some of our contemporaries publish a statement that General Sherman, in conversation with a lady in Fayetteville, said that if the results of his late visitation of the South did not restore its people to loyalty, he should, on his next invasion, burn every house to the ground, and if that did not work a cure he would put all the inhabitants to death, without regard to age or sex.

If you're tempted to think that this anecdote is unreliable or, again, hyperbole, think again. In the post-war period, Sherman reacted to an Indian massacre thus: "We must act with vindictive earnestness against the Sioux, even to their extermination, men, women, and children." General Sherman seemed to have a decent bit of genocidal ideation. In 1873 General Phillip Sheridan wrote to Sherman about his strategy for fighting Indians, and directly tied it to their mutual treatment of Southerners during the war:

> In taking the offensive [against Indians] I have to select that season when I can catch the fiends; and, if a village is attacked and women and children killed, the responsibility is not with the soldiers but with the people whose crimes necessitated the attack. During the war did anyone hesitate to attack a village or town occupied by the enemy because women or children

were within its limits? Did we cease to throw shells into Vicksburg or Atlanta because women and children were there?

In 1865 the prospect of any kind of fruitful reconciliation between the North and South seemed absolutely ludicrous. Hopeless. The dream of maniacs. Take a look around today. Signs and wonders, I dare say.

That is just political reconciliation. What about reconciliation between whites and blacks, former slave-owners and former slaves? Prospects for any kind of reconciliation between white and black in America were even bleaker than the prospects of political reconciliation between North and South. Take, for example, the renowned Southern Presbyterian theologian, Robert Louis Dabney. Dabney had served as Chaplain to General Stonewall Jackson, and was widely admired (and still is today in many circles). Dabney was a Christian gentleman, a servant of God, a leader in the Presbyterian church, and a learned man of the Word. Yet in 1867 he stood on the floor of the General Assembly of the Presbyterian Church and opposed the ordination of blacks. He did so with rhetoric that cannot be read without blushing. How ugly was it? Well, I don't want to spoil your appetite, but I will (especially on this day) because we need to collectively remember these things. The dark canvas I'm about to paint will allow us to see the signs and wonders in all their brilliance and glory.

Dabney argued:

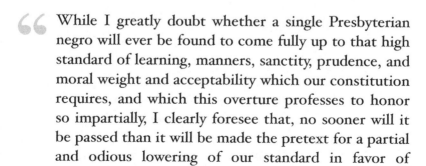 While I greatly doubt whether a single Presbyterian negro will ever be found to come fully up to that high standard of learning, manners, sanctity, prudence, and moral weight and acceptability which our constitution requires, and which this overture professes to honor so impartially, I clearly foresee that, no sooner will it be passed than it will be made the pretext for a partial and odious lowering of our standard in favor of

negroes [....] There has broken out among many a sort of morbid craving to ordain negroes—to get their hands on their heads.

And later:

> Now, who that knows the negro does not know that his is a subservient race; that he is made to follow, and not to lead; that his temperament, idiosyncrasy and social relation make him untrustworthy as a depository of power?

Or this:

> And now that every hope of the existence of church and of state, and of civilization itself, hangs upon our arduous efforts to defeat the doctrine of negro suffrage [...]

Or perhaps the most ugly passage of all:

> [O]nce political equality is confirmed to the blacks, every influence will tend towards that other consummation, *social equality*, which they will be so keen to demand, and their demagogues so ready to grant as the price of their votes [....] He must be 'innocent' indeed who does not see whither all this tends, as it is designed by our oppressors to terminate. It is (shall I pronounce the abhorred word?) to *amalgamation!* Yes, sir, these tyrants know that if they can mix the race of Washington and Lee and Jackson with the base herd which they brought from the fens of Africa, if they can taint the blood which hallowed the plains of Manassas with this sordid stream, the adulterous current will never again swell a Virginian's

heart with a throb noble enough to make a despot tremble. But they will then have, for all time, a race supple and groveling enough for all the purposes of oppression.

I know this is difficult, but bear with me for one last quote.

> Now then, gentlemen, come with me, and let us see whither this iron consistency in which you boast will lead us [....] [Y]ou must have this negro of yours reviewing and censuring the records of white sessions, and sitting to judge appeals brought before you by white parties, possibly even white ladies! [....] You made race and color no obstacle to putting this negro equal to yourselves [...] So there you have a black pastor to white families, clothed with official title to ask their experimental, heart secrets; to visit their sick beds; to celebrate baptisms, marriages and funerals over their children! And this, on your principle, is no Utopian picture, but what may become a literal fact in a month after you execute your plan.

Keep in mind these were the words of an otherwise exemplary Southern Christian gentleman. If that was how the *Christians* thought, what do you think the opinions were more broadly? As I say: racial equality and reconciliation? Absolutely hopeless.

It took a good bit longer for racial equality to materialize than it did political union. Dr. King lamented that the "promises" in the aftermath of the Civil War had not been fully realized a hundred years later. He argued that the Declaration of Independence was a promissory note: "All men are created equal and endowed by their Creator with certain inalienable rights, among which are life, liberty, and the pursuit of happiness." He and his followers in 1963, those gathered at the foot of the Lincoln Memorial, were there to peacefully demand payment.

WITH ALL THAT BACKGROUND, today I want you to stop and look around. The signs and wonders are so obvious and apparent one has to be utterly blind to not see it. God has been extravagantly gracious to this unique nation of ours. Where once racial and political equality was a dream only of "maniacs," today there are few who can read the words of a 19th century Southern theologian without cringing in abject horror.

That sort of turnaround does not happen on its own. It is not the natural order of things in this fallen world. It does not happen with good intentions. It does not happen by passing laws or social engineering. It is not the outcome of somebody just making a good argument. It happens because the God who raised Jesus Christ from the dead, the One who is "making all things new," really is at work in the world.

I know that people are often discouraged about lingering race issues in America.

As for me, I think the history of race relations in America is proof positive that God exists.

✸ 36 ✸

DON'T FORGET YOUR TOWEL

A memory from my youth.

In the spring of 1997 I boarded a Greyhound bus in Billings, Montana and traveled for over 65 hours to Lynchburg, Virginia. This took some serious dedication. I was a broke college student, but I really wanted to attend the graduation ceremony of my dear friend Beth, as well as to see a bunch of other friends I had met a few years earlier when I had attended their small Christian college.

In the fall of '94 and spring of '95 Beth and I had been almost inseparable. We were truly kindred spirits: similar interests, vivid imaginations, quick senses of wit, and just all-around enjoying being around one another. One of the things we mutually adored was Douglas Adams's magnificent comedy series, *The Hitchhiker's Guide to the Galaxy*. Our jokes and tales often incorporated themes from the *Hitchhiker's Guide*. She called me "Zaphod," after the character of Zaphod Beeblebrox, and I called her "Trillian," the nickname of the lead female character. Our friend Noah was "Arthur," after Arthur Dent.

Beth even sent me a blue towel once, monographed with "Zaphod."

This, of course, was one of the running jokes. The *Hitchhiker's Guide*, you see, is emphatic that the single most important rule for intergalactic travelers is to "never forget your towel." A towel has many uses. It can be a pillow for your head, a blanket for comfort, or you can use it to flag down passing spaceships to hitch a ride.

Anyway, I boarded the Greyhound to make the long trek to Lynchburg without telling Beth I was coming. In fact, I had told her that I wouldn't be attending the graduation. She understood, but I think was disappointed that I couldn't be there. When I finally arrived at the bus station in Lynchburg I was a filthy wreck. Showerless for days on end (as I said, it was a sixty-five *hour* bus ride), lacking sleep, I felt pretty greasy and grimy. My friend Noah picked me up and took me to the house he and a bunch of other guys rented.

After a shower and some dinner, I felt suitably revived, and part of that revival was the anticipation of putting my brilliant plan into action. We took off to a shopping center within two blocks of Beth's house, where I placed a call from a pay phone. (That is something that used to be ubiquitous in America, but has all but vanished. It is a free-standing telephone that you put loose change into in order to place a call.)

Beth picked up.

"Hey Trillian," I said. "This is Zaphod."

She was delighted at my call. We chitchatted about this and that.

Finally, "I'm really sorry I can't make it to your graduation."

"I know. Me too."

"Tell you what," I said. "When I hang up with you I'll take my towel outside and try to flag down a passing ship from the Vogon Constructor Fleet."

She laughed. "That would be really cool, wouldn't it?"

"Yes, it really would," I replied. "It's worth a shot, at least."

We said our goodbyes, and I wished her an awesome graduation with all her friends, and told her to say "hey" to them for me. She promised she would.

As soon as I hung up the phone, towel in hand I ran in a full sprint the two blocks to her house, where she and a bunch of other college girls were hanging out.

It took 45 seconds or a minute.

I bounded up the steps, trying to catch my breath, and immediately rang the doorbell.

Someone answered the door, but it wasn't Beth. I said, "Is Beth here?"

There was a bit of commotion and Beth came walking to the door from the living room. Her eyes glazed over and her jaw hit the floor.

"Hey Trillian," I said, holding up my Zaphod-inscribed towel. "What do you know? This thing actually *works!*"

Almost nothing in this world makes a 65-hour Greyhound ride worth it, but seeing the look on her face, I knew I'd found it.

✣ 37 ✣

PROVING GIAMATTI WRONG

I have always loved baseball writing. In the fall of 2003 the Philadelphia Phillies were in a pennant race, and it inspired me to make my contribution to this wonderful American genre. Two things particularly delight me in unearthing this essay: (1) my mention of the "rookie" Cabrera. He, of course, became one of the greatest hitters in baseball history. (2) Jim Thome's heroics. Years later—August 17th, 2010, to be exact—he would give me an even bigger thrill, this time for my beloved Minnesota Twins.

"It breaks your heart. It was meant to break your heart." So wrote late Commissioner A. Bartlett Giamatti, reflecting on how the game of baseball so utterly disappoints, yet continues to addict, its thousands of fans. It may well be true, but just the same it masks the occasional converse reality. In the case of a Philadelphia Phillies fan, that is a *very* occasional converse reality. George Will said it best: "The Phillies have had a bad century." I am undeterred.

Perhaps I'm affected by the weather. I always get sentimental and unduly emotional when Fall rolls around; it is just a melancholy time of year with its dark skies, swirling wind, leaves falling to the ground. All good songs are written in the autumn. It's late

September, and a hurricane is coming—Isabel, they call her. Already her outer bands like tentacles have invaded the skies and the winds buffet occasional sprays of rain. The news of her imminent arrival changed the game time, the original 7:05 rescheduled to 1:05. Good. I could catch the first pitch on the radio on my way home from class, and then I'd be able to catch some of it on TV before buttoning up my uniform and heading off to work.

We're in a playoff race—a *bona fide* playoff race. Okay, perhaps not really *bona fide* to true baseball purists. The Braves have long since run away with our division for the twelfth consecutive time. Disgusting. But we are hanging on to that newly invented breath of hope of which Giamatti never knew: the wildcard. Today is game three against our nemesis, the pesky and utterly infuriating Florida Marlins. We split the first two, today's the rubber game. Marlins lead us in the wildcard race by a game and a half. We have to win today. We have to. We "get" to play them again next week, only in Florida. But we always lose in Florida.

I'm in graduate school—theology. I had a class today, St. Paul's letter to the Romans. I asked our august professor mid-hour, somewhat tongue-in-cheek: "Moving on to the really important things... do you think the Phillies can pull it out?" Never one to duck crucial questions, he pinched his chin with his fingers and frowned. "Where were you in 1950?" he asked me. "In the mind of God," I shot back. "Well, I was a little further along than that, and given our history things don't look too promising." Leave it to him to match his baseball passion with his eschatology. He and the ghost of Giamatti. What does he know? Being right about St. Paul doesn't make you right about baseball. I need a little more optimism.

Class is out, I'm cruising home. Radio's on. Oh, I forgot. *We're facing Willis.* He's this young, powerful lefty—a rookie, but dominating. "The D-Train" they call him. That kind of hype always rubs me the wrong way, but he seems like a pretty nice kid. He's the front-runner for the Rookie of the Year award. We're doomed, I think. His hitless inning on the way home won't change that opinion.

The screen door shuts behind me, I say 'hi' to my wife, who's busy in the kitchen. I quickly get the game on TV, go upstairs to get my baseball buddy—she's eleven months. Last night—I swear—she said exactly her *fourth* word. "Kitty" was first. Then came "Daddy," which comes out a hilarious "Da-duh." "Momma" is a rarely used third. Last night when the game was on, she pointed her finger at the screen and said, "Bay-bah." She did it four times, that kid. Who ever heard of "baseball" as a fourth word? She's overjoyed to see me—does her little scrunch up of her neck, mouth wide-open smile. A quick kiss for Daddy, then we're down in the La-Z-Boy watching the game like always. She even claps as daddy teaches her new cheers.

Not much to cheer about. Millwood's on the hill for us. He's our ace, but he's been an inconsistent one. He was a big off-season pickup for us, a major *coup* from those Braves, who from the looks of it don't appear to be too disturbed about it. But he's sharp today. Maybe Isabel's wind—now ruffling the umpire's pants—is helping that nasty breaker snap a bit more. Trouble in the fourth, though. Millie had been able to get out of a two-on, no out jam in the third, but the Fish won't let you make that mistake twice. They put three on the board. 3-0. Facing Willis, that's not good.

Grilled-cheese sandwiches and soup for lunch. Boy is it that kind of day; and with the weather closing in, I know it's destined to go even further south—one of the hazards of baseball in September. I just hope if they have to call the game early we're in the lead...

We catch a nice break in the fifth. Tomas Perez, our second baseman, finally gets us on the board with a nice line-drive into the left field bullpen. So, the D-Train is fallible after all. But the inning isn't over yet. With two outs we manage to scratch and claw to get runners on first and second, and Mike Lieberthal steps in. He's our catcher, and what a year he's had with runners on. He shoots a little flare pop up down the right field line—a true chest deflator. But wait! Isabel gives the ball a little push toward right field and the first baseman reaches over his head...has it...no! Our runners, both going on the pitch, come around to score. Tie game. Relief.

Every time we score a couple runs lately the Fish inevitably come back and bite us the next inning. But Millwood, determined to stop that trend, fires and mows down the first two batters of the sixth. Boy he's got that curveball crackling today. He's got the rookie Cabrera in the hole 0-2 now. The next pitch is a mistake. Watching the replay they show him come out of the wind-up, throw the ball and almost immediately thrust his fists toward the ground in frustration, mouthing a word probably not fit to print. He never even looks at where the ball goes. He knows. Marlins on top again, 4-3.

Just now a little rain starts to fall. *Come on, Izzie, hold off just long enough for us to get the lead!* How long will we make her wait?

At least longer than the sixth. We come up short and outs are running out. The seventh inning arrives, and I'm getting antsy because I've got to get ready for work. But I can't pull myself away from the action. I finally turn the volume up loud enough to hear upstairs, and head up to change clothes. I make it quick. We manage to keep them off the board for the top half, but suffer two quick outs in the bottom half.

I'm gathering my stuff together, my backpack, coffee thermos, coffee cup, bag of dinner, water bottle – the essentials for a long night at work. All this while hardly taking my eyes off the screen. Polanco is up—Polly, the team calls him—our last hope for the seventh. I'm wondering how he's feeling. Guy's been playing Gold Glove infield for us all year, batting near .300, only to be sidelined the past two weeks with a hamstring pull. Is he rusty? Do guys on the DL even do batting practice? These questions unconsciously swirl around my head. *Crrrack!* My eyes shoot up to the screen—I have been briefly distracted—and I see a bullet line-drive toward left-center. He hit it hard. It only took but a second to clear the fence. Tie game again. This is going to be a gut-wrencher.

I'm in the car again, fighting the traffic for five miles heading to work. I had kissed my girls goodbye with the usual fanfare, but Tara nudged me on. She says, "Get out to the car so you can listen on the radio!" She's become a fan. The drive is its normal, miserable animal. Fighting traffic, red lights every fifty yards, seems like. It's very dark for three o'clock, a little bit of rain drifts down, slickening the asphalt. But I lie. I don't remember the drive at all. I remember the sound of the crowd—only twenty thousand due to the time change and weather, but still strong—the slap of the ball hitting the catcher's mitt (the radio guys must put microphones down on the field to get that effect), the occasional *pop!* of the ball being fouled out of play. I hear the emotion in Scott Graham's voice as he calls the play-by-play. He's as nervous as me. Our color guy, Chris Wheeler, is truly beside himself.

Top-eight. I feel a little better now that Cormier's on the mound. He has been unbelievable this year, an ERA that seems like its under 1.00. He's on-form today. He's a lefty, has a very crafty delivery, great location on his fastball, and a killer split for his "out" pitch. Two outs and a man on, the batter scorches a line drive down the third base line...but Polly—*it's great to have YOU back*—is guarding the line in a "no-doubles" defense and snares the wicked hit.

Mid-inning, I listen to all the usual radio advertisements. If you listen to enough games, you get really, really sick of the same ads over and over: a car dealership, a local bank, hot dogs, buns and rolls, a cacophony of the most obnoxious voices radio can find. Over the last few games I've been in the habit of switching stations instead of enduring the torture. Not today. I can't afford to miss a pitch.

Bottom of the eighth and Jim Thome is up. He played for the Cleveland Indians for about 12 seasons, I think, and I know him from growing up a Twins fan. He was nothing less than a Twins-killer, which is the reason I've always hated his guts. But now he's on *my* team, and I've since discovered that perhaps I don't hate him as much as I hate any successful Cleveland team. The Phillies picked him up as a free agent in the off-season, sweetening the pot to some ungodly number of dollars. For the most part, he's paid off. He's one home run back of Bonds right now; that's saying something. But one thing about picking up great sluggers: unless their name is Barry Bonds, you always have to deal with the strikeouts.

Oh yes, the strikeouts. In Jim Thome's case, something like 170 of them.

At least it's a new pitcher—we finally knocked the D-Train out of the game. Thome steps in the batter's box. *"Swing and a miss!"* I hear the call. That's okay, I tell myself. He's swinging first pitch fastball and got a slider instead. No problem. Pause. *"Swwwinngg and a miss!"* I hear again. Oh boy. Thome is terrible in 0-2 counts— his prime strikeout count. I could call the next pitch long before it came. It's signature, and every pitcher in the league knows it: Thome is a sucker for high fastballs. He can't lay off of them. I'm probably breaking the first rule you learn in driver's training right now: never drive when you're stressed out. "The set... the 0-2 pitch... lays off a high fastball!" I can hardly believe it. Nor can I believe it when he lays off *the next two* fastballs. Full count. The 3-2 pitch is on the way...

The *"crack"* registers in my head. I hear the roar of the crowd. My throat sinks down into my stomach and I can feel the adrenaline pump into every limb. All this in the millisecond between the sound and the moment Scott Graham makes the call, *"DEEP DRIVE TO RIGHT CENTER..."*—my knuckles whiten as they grip the steering wheel—*"TO THE TRACK..."*—my foot is a little too heavy on the gas pedal—*"TO THE WALL..."*—every muscle tensed —*"LOOKING UP...THAT BALL IS GONE!!!"*

I can hear the crowd, frenzied. It's enough to make a grown man choke up. Trust me. I know. Pumping my fist, completely despising my past, I mutter to myself, "I love you Jim Thome, I love you Jim Thome, I love you Jim Thome. You're worth every penny." The commentator, caught up in the moment, emphatically asks a rhetorical question, "Do you want some DRAMA here at Veteran's Stadium?" He shouldn't have asked that. Spoils the drama. Oh well, it's dramatic nonetheless. And I thought our color guy was beside himself *before* the hit.

Cormier pitches the ninth. That's been another problem this season: having our veteran closer have a near complete mechanical and mental breakdown going down the stretch. It's hard to get into the playoffs without a closer. But Cormier quickly guns down the pinch hitter and the lead-off man. One out to go. The count runs up to full. The crowd is standing, getting louder. "As if on cue," the commentator reports, the spectator everyone forgot about for the past inning makes her appearance. Isabel starts kicking up the wind. The rains come down. The set...the pitch... "pops him up...."

I KNOW AS WELL as my seasoned theology professor the reality. I know that we don't play well in Florida. I know that the final series of the season has us playing the seemingly unbeatable Braves while the Marlins play the all-but-pathetic New York Mets. In my heart of hearts, I know that Bart Giamatti was right: the game was meant to break my heart. Then why do I come back? Why do I know that tomorrow, faithful as ever, and the next day and the day after, I will be glued to my radio or television set, determined to follow every pitch to the bitter end? I know all the realities, but now I also know something else.

Today Giamatti was wrong.

❧ 38 ❧

ON GRACE & LEISURE

The Christian church has a mixed track record when it comes to encouraging industry and entrepreneurialism. The economic marketplace and business pursuits have often been considered a lesser pursuit—honorable, perhaps, but not a sacred vocation in the full sense of that term. Many Christian communities apply great pressure and guilt on people engaged in business pursuits, either by encouraging them to dedicate themselves to "full time ministry" or by implying that the sole legitimate purpose of their pursuits is to fund so-called "full time ministry," as though their purposes ought to be reduced to purely utilitarian benefits to the church. Our Christian bookshelves are overflowing nowadays with books on how to live a properly "radical" Christian life or how not to "waste" one's life; generally, they mean eschewing a life of such lowly pursuits as making and enjoying a good living.

There has emerged in recent years a healthy reaction in the other direction: a high-octane theology of the sheer goodness of work, labor, creativity, entrepreneurialism, economics, business pursuits, and the human flourishing to which they contribute. After all, these things are all aspects of our very humanity as the image of God. Cultivating, ruling, and subduing, applying all our powers of ingenuity, creativity, and reason to the raw stuff of nature, and—yes —reaping the rewards of our labors is an integral part of what it means to be human. It is not a lesser calling, much less a "necessary evil."

As needed as this corrective may be, it carries with it other dangers—dangers to which Americans seem particularly suscepti- ble. In 1840 Alexis de Tocqueville, the famous foreign observer of American affairs, wrote:

> In America I saw the freest and most enlightened men placed in the happiest circumstances that the world affords; it seemed to me as if a cloud habitually hung upon their brow, and I thought them serious and almost sad, even in their pleasures [...] The chief reason [is that they] are forever brooding over advantages they do not possess. It is strange to see with what feverish ardor the Americans pursue their own welfare, and to watch the vague dread that constantly torments them lest they should not have chosen the shortest path which may lead to it.

As much as work and industry is a good gift of God, we would be foolish to think that they cannot become objects of idolatry. Put plainly: there is a reason the term "workaholic" exists. As Tocqueville observed of 19th century Americans, idolatries never satisfy; they ironically keep the object of our deepest desires always elusive. We work so that we may enjoy, but the worship of work precludes genuine enjoyment.

It would be a shame if the inspiration of entrepreneurialism for the glory of God were to miss out on a crucial aspect of that very glory. The God who created the heavens and the earth also rested and declared it all "very good." Part of being his image and likeness, part of reflecting his glory, is that we not only learn to work and labor, but that we learn what it is to truly rest and affirm. Work without true rest, writes Josef Pieper, "can only be compared to the labors of Sisyphus, that mythical symbol of the 'worker' chained to his function, never pausing in his work, and never gathering any fruit from his labors." (*Leisure: The Basis of Culture* [Ignatius, 2009]: 69)

∿

THE IDOLIZING of work has a long history in the western world. As much as the early titans of industry preached work as the preeminent virtue (the better, one might cynically say, to maximize the productivity of their laborers), the Marxist critique hardly represented an alternative. Its idealized human being is the "proletarian," the "worker." Marx's reduction of the human being to *homo economicus* was actually a maximizing, not minimizing. Proletarians in a "Worker's Paradise" are people wholly tied to the all-consuming system of labor.

It is this context of modernism's idolatry of work to which philosopher Josef Pieper directed his brilliant 1952 essay, "Leisure: The Basis of Culture." He views this worldview of "total work," the elevation of labor as the preeminent human virtue, as fundamentally dehumanizing. If the miserable fruits of Marxism's various attempts at Proletarian revolutions are not enough evidence, consider the symbol found on the gates of Auschwitz: *Arbeit Macht Frei*—"Work makes you free." Dehumanizing, indeed. Yet idolatry is equal opportunity with its victims. Even the prosperous, liberty-loving west produces slaves; people chained to their desks, obsessed with what they do not possess, and characterized by what Tocqueville calls a "vague dread."

Pieper writes that the modern notion of work and worker expresses "a new and changing conception of the nature of man, a new and changing conception of the very meaning of human existence" (22). These claims raise the stakes to rather monumental proportions. Is it really true that what we think about work entails an entire worldview?

Idolatry always involves the corruption of something good. It is parasitic. It does not exist on its own; it cannot exist without taking goods and twisting them to violate the First Commandment: "You shall have no other gods before me." So here: Work, in itself, is good. Adam and Eve were called to "rule and subdue" the natural world in unspoiled Eden. But what happens when we believe, ever so subtly, that this activity constitutes the essence of humanity, its greatest good, and its highest aspiration? A number of things: It corrupts how we value things: only the fruits of our restless activity become important. This makes rest and leisure impossible, for they are not the results of our activity—they are the opposite of work and effort. In turn, we are led to a kind of stultifying narcissism that destroys our capacity for charity, both giving and receiving. Let us consider both.

IN DEUTERONOMY 8:17-18, God warns the Israelites of the temptation to believe that their newfound prosperity in the promised land is the result of their own activity and achievements:

 You may say to yourself, 'My power and the strength of my hands have produced this wealth for me.' But remember the LORD your God, for it is he who gives you the ability to produce wealth, and so confirms his covenant, which he swore to your forefathers, as it is today.

It is a simple fact that hard work produces good things; and it is therefore all too natural for us to then attribute prosperity solely to our activity or efforts. This deception is as subtle as it is destructive. When we believe that value is caused exclusively—or even primarily—by the amount of our active effort involved in something, we are really proclaiming our autonomy: "My power and the strength of my hands have produced this wealth for me." Who hasn't to some extent felt this? That the value of something is directly measured by how much effort we put into it?

If activity and effort exclusively produces value, is it any wonder that the workaholic looks derisively at leisure? There is no room for any measure of passivity—that is how he defines laziness. And when rest and leisure are attempted by such a person it is merely as a necessary evil, a purely utilitarian function to "recharge" the batteries so that one can, as soon as possible, get back to doing important and valuable things. But if leisure is reduced to a function, a tool used to serve our active pursuits, it ceases to be leisure; it has been co-opted as the slave of activity, work to be done in order to work. It is doubtful such a person will ever reap the benefits of true leisure—passivity, rest, contemplation—because he or she doesn't really believe it has benefits of its own. It isn't a product of labor. Value is the product of effort, nothing more, and nothing less. There is no room for "effortlessness" in this frame of mind. This is why the modern person has so many things he or she describes as "guilty pleasures." Guilty of what, exactly? Enjoying something as a pure gift, without exertion, effort, or "deserving" it. And a guilty conscience is not—indeed, cannot be—a leisurely conscience.

So Pieper observes,

> The inmost significance of the exaggerated value which is set upon hard work appears to be this: man seems to mistrust everything that is effortless; he can only enjoy, with a good conscience, what he has acquired with toil and trouble; he refuses to have anything as a gift (35-6).

This is how idolatry of work destroys charity. Not just the obvious and mundane fact that workaholics tend to think the less fortunate lazy and not entitled to their charity; the worker himself is incapable of receiving charity. I know people like this, and perhaps you do as well. The workaholic, the type of person who has the first dollar they ever made framed over the mantlepiece, the self-made man, the independent and successful woman—these are the types of proud people who never accept charity or help.

But it runs far deeper than the refusal to let someone pick up a restaurant tab. The idolatry of activity and work shrinks us; our entire outlook is shriveled and constrained by our new value system which essentially says the world—or at least that which is important in the world—is what we make it to be by our efforts. Our souls are never receptive, passive, or "open" to things outside ourselves and our control. Rather, we become obsessed with control, activity, power, and manipulation—"subduing" the earth quickly turns into a mandate to subdue everything. This is why you have rarely met a workaholic who is not simultaneously a "control freak." They lack the capacity to passively gaze in admiration, appreciation, and wonder at a world outside their competence or control.

And this gets to the very heart of it. What is at stake is the reality of grace. Pieper suggests that if we do not value things which are "not due to the effort of man, [then] there is nothing gratuitous [...], nothing 'inspired,' nothing 'given' [...]"(30). Is there such a thing as a gift? Is creation itself a gift, or some kind of merited necessity? If there is a "givenness" to reality which we merely encounter (not create), then it is something we are meant to receive with simple thankfulness. Or, on the other hand, are we the primary creators of reality, value, and dignity?

At bottom this question is nothing less than the titanic ancient battle between Pelagius and Augustine. For Pelagius, whatever we achieve is by our own autonomous wills; the world is run by work and by works. There is nothing to be received, only things to be achieved. Augustine responded with the biblical— indeed, Deuteronomic—vision: the cosmos is radiated by divine grace—an act of God "prior to" our works. "It is the Lord who gives you the ability to produce wealth." The workaholic, the idolater of effort and labor, is a Pelagian at heart. He does not possess the requisite virtues by which to engage in true leisure. And, like all Pelagians, he is tormented by guilt if he does attempt it, for it requires that he not work or perform. The workaholic does not know how to receive because he does not properly know the grace of God.

Leisure is celebration. It is a receptive affirmation, praise, and enjoyment of a world outside ourselves and our efforts. Pieper calls it "a receptive attitude of mind, a contemplative attitude, and it is not only the occasion but also the capacity for steeping oneself in the whole of creation" (47). What a wonderful metaphor: a teabag is "steeped." It absorbs its surroundings and passively influences them. And, mind you, steeping oneself in the "whole" of creation means paying attention to a great many things with which our efforts and activity have nothing to do. The workaholic knows of no such world. Leisure is the safeguard against the shriveled narcissism of "me, myself, and I." Leisure is ultimately a way of being formed and shaped by grace, a reminder that we have not achieved our prosperity by our own hands, but by a gratuitous and unmerited act of God.

If Augustine and Pelagius are too high brow, consider two simple women: Mary and Martha. Martha

> had a sister called Mary, who sat at the Lord's feet listening to what he said. But Martha was distracted by all the preparations that had to be made. She came to him and asked, 'Lord, don't you care that my sister has left me to do the work by myself? Tell her to help me!' 'Martha, Martha,' the Lord answered, 'you are worried and upset about many things, but only one thing is needed. Mary has chosen what is better, and it will not be taken away from her' (Luke 10:39-42).

Beware your works and your efforts, even efforts done for the

Lord; works proceed from grace. And grace is received, not achieved. At the feet of Jesus.

So what begins as a subtle deception becomes, in the end, nothing short of a war against God. This ought to be expected, for it was so in the Garden of Eden. The Serpent was subtle and cunning, and a small thing—eating fruit, taking by one's own hand instead of receiving with gladness all that God had provided—ended with disastrous consequences. We who are motivated to restore work to its proper place of dignity, should take special care to avoid turning it into idolatry. Pieper again:

> [T]he central problem of liberating men from [being fettered to the process of work] lies in making a whole field of significant activity available and open to the working man—of activity which is not 'work'; in other words: in making the sphere of real leisure available to him (63).

It turns out that God has provided just such a sphere.

～

THE FIRST CHAPTER of Genesis provides our foundation, where we discover that God ended the work which he had made and, "behold, it was very good." Being the image of God means that we, too, celebrate the end of our works and reflect and dwell on the reality of creation—not merely what we have accomplished, but all that God has done. This creational pattern forms the image-bearing pattern:

> Remember the Sabbath day by keeping it holy. Six days you shall labor and do all your work, but the seventh day is a Sabbath to the LORD your God. On it you shall not do any work, neither you, nor your son or daughter, nor your manservant or maidservant, nor

your animals, nor the alien within your gates. For in six days the LORD made the heavens and the earth, the sea, and all that is in them, but he rested on the seventh day. Therefore the LORD blessed the Sabbath day and made it holy. (Exodus 20:8-11)

I will be honest. In my four decades as a Christian I have read and listened to countless treatments of this famous text, mostly by very strict people telling me why I should not throw a ball or go fly-fishing on Sunday. In most instances, their main argument amounts to a pure divine command defense: "God said it. Now, obey." While that may well be true, it does tend to give the impression that this command is just arbitrary, as though there is no rationale for it and that it could have been otherwise. So occasionally it might be supplemented with other purely utilitarian reasons like, "God knew you needed rest, and so he provided it." But rarely is there an explanation of any purposes grander than this. Now, I am aware that the 4th Commandment to keep the Sabbath Day (or what became known as the "Lord's Day" in the New Testament era) and what it might precisely mean for Christians has been hotly contested. I make no attempt to settle the question, but I do offer a few things to consider.

If it is true that idolatry of work restricts our view only to that for which we expend effort or control, and only ascribe value to things with reference to our effort, then in a very real sense we are pretending to be God, surveying only the works of our hands and declaring those "very good." And if, as Pieper suggests, what we need is a sphere of real leisure, a space and time where we break free from our obsession with ourselves, it seems to me that we are provided such a sphere directly in the creation account itself with God's blessing of the Sabbath Day.

If this is true then leisure is not a supplement or "add on" to human nature, something to be done while feeling guilty about it. It is not a utilitarian "necessary evil" for the mere purpose of regaining energy to redouble our efforts. On the contrary, far from being an arbitrary thing, leisure is something we are positively designed for. It is the setting aside of time to not be obsessed with our works, but to "steep ourselves in the whole world," giving thanks to its Creator.

~

THE FOUNDATION OF TRUE LEISURE, therefore, is in worship. This is the meaning of Sabbath rest. Sabbath rest is to time what the temple was to space. A temple is an intentional clearing and sanctifying of space, a place that is the opposite of utility—it is not "useful." In fact, it is sacrilege to use this space for one's own purposes. It is rather a space where one is confronted with and receives transcendent reality. Likewise, the setting aside of a day is the intentional clearing and sanctifying of time—time that is not "useful" in the ordinary sense of the word. It is a time when work and effort are laid aside in contemplative and receptive affirmation of transcendence. A day of rest and leisure, in other words, is a design feature for God's finite image bearers. One that, neglected, leads to self-centeredness, an incapacity to appreciate grace and charity, and, of course, burnout, for we are not gods. We are not infinite and omnipotent. Seen in this light, the leisure time God has provided for his image bearers is not really a negotiable thing. And I wonder if our—and I certainly include myself here—widespread ambivalence to the 4th Commandment is itself an indication that we are already in idolatry's grip.

There is one other paramount consideration. It is a curious irony that sin always obtains precisely the opposite of its promises, and this is no less true with the idolatry of work. A life wholly consumed with work promises wealth, but in fact it cannot produce true wealth. For wealth, by definition, is superfluous—it is above and beyond the realm of necessity. But the moment such a thing appears in the life of one obsessed with work, he wonders, "What shall I *do* with it? How can I *use* this?" It is immediately seized upon and made to serve utilitarian ends, rather than being passively received as an end in itself. At the very moment it emerges from the grinding world of work, it is dragged right back into it. To put it another way, if all dividends are just reinvested, they simply accumulate and they are never enjoyed. "Wealth" that is never enjoyed is not worthy of the name.

Worship, on the other hand, creates real wealth because sacrifice is at the heart of it. And sacrifice is an offering freely given—questions like "Is it useful to me?" do not arise with such sacrifice. Pieper brilliantly observes:

> The act of worship creates a store of real wealth that cannot be consumed by the workaday world. It sets up an area where calculation is thrown to the winds and goods are deliberately squandered, where usefulness is forgotten and generosity reigns. Such wastefulness is, we repeat, true wealth; the wealth of the festival time. And only in this festival time can leisure unfold and come to fruition (68).

And God has given us a festival time—one a week, to be precise. If we want to experience real wealth, overflowing bounty not constrained by usefulness or calculation, we would do well to celebrate this day.

~

MAKE LEISURE A PRIORITY. Leisure is basking in grace: receiving with thankfulness, not achieving with sweat and tears. Leisure is the realm of real wealth—that is, generosity and hospitality freely given. It is the antithesis of narcissistic self-interest. Proverbs 23:7 puts a fine point on it:

Do not eat the food of a stingy man,
do not crave his delicacies;
for he is the kind of man
who is always thinking about the cost.

'Eat and drink,' he says to you,
but his heart is not with you.
You will vomit up the little you have eaten
and will have wasted your compliments.

It seems to me that the Christian church has often looked at leisure just as suspiciously as it has the world of business, work, and industry. I mentioned the plethora of books and resources that speak of being "radical" Christians; and their authors sometimes idolize work just as much as the worldly workaholic, only it is, like Martha, the work of ministry to which they are committed. Leisure is often despised in these books as a waste of precious time and something that should be engaged in as little as possible, just enough to recover enough energy to go on being "radical." And it is no accident that these books tend to produce guilt in their readers, who are left wondering how they, too, can be as industrious and serious and energetic as these radicals who throw themselves with abandon into "full time" ministry and reject the material comforts of life. They cause guilt because there is a subtle Pelagianism lying just underneath the surface: what is valuable is directly measured by our effort.

On the contrary, what is valuable is a gift. It is God's grace. And leisure is receiving and affirming and thanking God for his gifts, not trying to earn them, add to them, or subtract from them.

Do not judge God's gifts by their usefulness to you or—even worse—their usefulness to him. That is the way of Judas: "Why wasn't this perfume sold and the money given to the poor?" Just receive them with gratitude and thanksgiving. It is too-rarely noticed that in the Apostle Paul's seminal diagnosis of rebellious humanity in Romans 1, the first manifestation of idolatry is not sexual deviance. It is, rather, that "they neither glorified him as God nor *gave him thanks*." Thanklessness is the deepest, primal fruit of idolatry. Leisure is above all a sphere, a posture, and act of thankfulness. In it we exercise our innate capacity to receive from God.

In his book, *Thanks!* (Houghton Mifflin Harcourt, 2007), Robert Emmons quotes Elizabeth Bartlett's account of her response to her debilitating illness:

> [I]t is not enough for me to be thankful. I have a desire to do something in return. To do thanks. To give thanks. Give things. Give thoughts. Give love. So gratitude becomes the gift, creating a cycle of giving and receiving, the endless waterfall. Filling up and spilling over. To give from the fullness of my being. This comes not from a feeling of obligation, like a child's obligatory thank-you notes to grandmas and aunts and uncles after receiving presents. Rather, it is a spontaneous charitableness, perhaps not even to the giver but to someone else, to whoever crosses one's path. It is the simple passing on of the gift.

∾

IF LEISURE IS a receptive affirmation of God's gifts, it also means that leisure is as broad as the range of God's gifts. There is no "one size fits all" here. Your leisure time will reflect the blessings God bestows in your life for you to receive and enjoy. My leisure often includes a trout stream and a fly rod. One of the reasons the Lord's Day has fallen on hard times, it seems to me, is that many churches reduced the day to a sterile, stultifying uniformity and subjected it to infinite calculations about what we cannot do—and uniformity is not the kind of thing for which we were created.

That said, we do know that leisure flows from worship, and so worship should characterize the day. The writer of Hebrews exhorts us: "Let us not give up meeting together, as some are in the habit of doing, but let us encourage one another—and all the more as you see the Day approaching" (10:25). If we get this one thing right—the worship of our God of grace in the fellowship of believers—it will shape and form us. It will increase our capacity as receptive creatures to truly lay aside our labors and, with wild abandon, all calculation thrown to the wind, enjoy and share with sheer delight all that God has given us.

That is true wealth.

39

THE SCOURING OF THE SHIRE: IN DEFENSE OF UNTIDY ENDINGS

A Christmas Essay.

[Scour, v. To clean or brighten the surface (of something) by rubbing it hard, typically with an abrasive or detergent.]

'I shan't call it the end, till we've cleared up the mess,' said Sam gloomily. 'And that'll take a lot of time and work.'

Peter Jackson's cinematic re-telling of J.R.R. Tolkien's *The Return of the King* is known for its multiple endings, and each is pleasant enough. Healing, courtship, weddings, coronation, tributes, celebrations, departures and returns, the message is clear: war is over. There is at last a King in Gondor, and evil is destroyed.

Most visually stunning is the return of the four hobbit heroes to the Shire. Following the dark, brooding color palette of Mordor, the lush green is a sight for sore eyes. Frodo, Sam, Merry, and Pippin find their homeland just as they remembered it. Life goes on in the Shire, full of cheer, pipe-weed, and beer. There is no more conflict. Oh, there is a kind of sadness among the four as nostalgia sets in, along with a kind of regret that their neighbors are quite incapable of knowing the full significance of their exploits. Things will never quite be the same because they themselves are not the same. But all told, Jackson finishes his nearly ten-hour epic by returning to pastoral scenes and the deep, satisfying peace of Sam's final words to Rosie: "Well, I'm back."

Tolkien's version is not nearly so tidy, which can be a let-down to casual readers and an irritant to CGI-loving directors of blockbuster films. Compared to the terror of Helm's Deep or the thrill of Pelennor Fields, the 'Battle of Bywater, 1419' (as it is known to posterity), is a decidedly parochial affair. No orcs, goblins, trolls, Nazgul, or Oliphaunts, just a few Hobbits subduing a gang of ruffians under the command of Captains Meriadoc Brandybuck and Peregrin Took. The "Scouring of the Shire" (as Tolkien's chapter is called) may not be an expected or convenient ending, but it has the merit of being true.

What am I saying? True? It is fiction, to be sure. But there is Truth here, with a capital "T." Truth that (cinematic run times notwithstanding) should be neither skipped nor changed.

~

 The travelers trotted on, and as the sun began to sink towards the White Downs far away on the western horizon they came to Bywater by its wide pool; and there they had their first really painful shock. This was Frodo and Sam's own country, and they found out now that they cared about it more than any other place in the world. Many of the houses that they had known were missing. Some seemed to have been burned down. The pleasant row of old hobbit-holes in the bank on the north side of the Pool were deserted, and their little gardens that used to run down bright to the water's edge were rank with weeds. Worse, there was a whole line of the ugly new houses all along Pool Side, where the Hobbiton Road ran close to the bank. An avenue of trees had stood there. They were all gone. And looking with dismay up the road towards Bag End they saw a tall chimney of brick in the distance. It was pouring out black smoke into the evening air.

THE FOUR HEROIC hobbits do not return to the Shire of their memories. It is not lush and green. The pipe-weed is all missing (having been sent to Saruman's stores in Isengard), the taverns are closed, and beer is banned. The only thing there is no shortage of is "rules," as new and ever-lengthening signage informs them, and which they promptly tear down in contempt. Old Gaffer Gamgee comically explains how dire is his personal situation:

> 'While you've been trapesing in foreign parts, chasing Black Men up mountains from what my Sam says, though what for he don't make clear, they've been and dug up Bagshot Row and ruined my taters!'

The full reality is not so comical. At their first meeting with a gang of ruffians Frodo says, "Much has happened since you left the South. The Dark Tower has fallen, and there is a King in Gondor." Yet here they stand dumbstruck at the Dark Tower in miniature looming over Bag End: a brick chimney belching black smoke. Here someone called "Chief" lords it over the Shire, not the one enthroned in Minas Tirith.

> 'This is worse than Mordor!' said Sam. 'Much worse in a way. It comes home to you, as they say; because it is home, and you remember it before it was all ruined.'
> 'Yes, this is Mordor,' said Frodo. 'Just one of its works.'

This is not the sentimental and satisfying return of the cinematic version. Why is Tolkien dragging this out? Do we really need another battle? Is this one of those Victor Hugo chapters, the ones that make you think he's being paid by the word? Daniel Defoe, inventor of the English novel, frankly botched the ending of his otherwise brilliant *Robinson Crusoe* by throwing in one last, completely superfluous adventure. He just couldn't help himself, as further evidenced by his literarily disastrous sequel, *The Farther Adventures of Robinson Crusoe*. As the saying goes, quit while you're ahead. Is Tolkien falling for Dafoe's brand of self-indulgence here?

Hardly. He knows the Truth too well. Breaking the power of Mordor does not suddenly (as Peter Jackson would have it) transform the world into a Thomas Kinkade painting. In the official annals of Middle Earth found in Appendix B of the *Lord of the Rings*, Tolkien records this remarkable line:

> November 3 (3019, Shire Reckoning 1419). Battle of Bywater, and Passing of Saruman. End of the War of the Ring.

Think of that. The destruction of the Ring and the downfall of Sauron was not the end of the "War of the Ring?" Not to Tolkien's way of thinking. The wounds must heal (and forever leave scars, as Frodo would find) and the destruction must be repaired. The "works of Mordor," to use Frodo's phrase, must be dealt with, along with the servants of Mordor; in the immediate case, that means Saruman.

Tolkien calls it "scouring." It is an unfolding process, implicit in Sam's wonderful way of putting it in his question to Gandalf: *"Is everything sad going to come untrue?"* Sadness must be made untrue, and that is not done by just wishing it or emoting, as Merry chidingly reminds Frodo:

> 'But if there are many of these ruffians,' said Merry, 'it will certainly mean fighting. You won't rescue Lotho, or the Shire, just by being shocked and sad, my dear Frodo.'

Scouring is needed. Detergent must be applied, even into hard-to-reach places like the Shire. There may be a King in faraway Gondor, but his rule must be felt.

> [Pippin] cast back his cloak, flashed out his sword, and the silver and sable of Gondor gleamed on him as he rode forward. 'I am a messenger of the King,' he said. 'You are speaking to the King's friend, and one of the most renowned in all the lands of the West. You are a ruffian and fool. Down on your knees in the road and ask pardon, or I will set this troll's bane in you!'

～

TOLKIEN KNEW this from personal experience, of course, having served in the dreary and miserable trenches of World War One. That explains his hatred of barren wastelands (Mordor), heavy machinery (Isengard), and black smoke. But I think it's more than the story of his experience. Behind it lies the bigger story, the one he famously called the "true myth": the grand narrative of creation and redemption culminating in Jesus of Nazareth.

It is no accident that the Fellowship's journey from Rivendell begins on Christmas Day, the dawn of December 25th. Neither is it incidental that when Frodo Baggins and Samwise Gamgee at long last struggle up the slopes of Mount Doom to destroy Sauron by way of the One Ring, it is March 25th, the traditional ecclesiastical date of Good Friday.

Tolkien's story is framed by the liturgical calendar, and so the Shire's scouring is not superfluous. After all, in the "true myth," Easter victory did not instantly transform the world. The enthronement of the King of kings and Lord of lords had to be announced by his messengers to those kings and lords in distant places, "in Jerusalem, and in all Judea and Samaria, and to the ends of the earth."

‟ 'The King's Messengers will ride up the Greenway now, not bullies from Isengard.'—Frodo Baggins

∾

THE SCOURING of the Shire is one of my favorite chapters. In an obvious sense, it is a simple coming-of-age story. The meek and terrified hobbits, now fully matured and steeled by their adventures, return home and exercise wisdom and leadership without the direct aid of Gandalf the White or Aragorn, son of Arathorn. It is also the story of Saruman's end; fittingly, by the vengeful blade of his pitiful, abused servant Wormtongue. Black is black, evil is evil, and spreads the same tyranny, black smoke, and misery wherever it goes, even into the pastures and woodlands of the Shire.

But most of all it is a reminder that Mordor has stained everything. Nothing is exempt, not even our most cherished places. *"It comes home to you,"* Sam remarks, *"because it is home."* Evil corrupted even the most idyllic corner of Middle Earth. The victory is won, but we *"shan't call it the end till we've cleared up the mess."* The world must be scoured, cleaned, mended, and healed. As great as were the crumbling of Barad-dur, the sacking of Isengard by the Ents, the shriek of the Witch-King of Arnor under the blade of Eowyn of Rohan, there remains the small but no less important matter of Bagshot Row and Old Gaffer's ruined taters.

Tolkien got it right. Christmas and Easter together do not spell "the end." There is much work to do. Our own homes, relationships, vocations, thoughts, desires, inclinations, and hearts must be scoured and healed by the good news of a new King. Gandalf says, *"The hands of the king are the hands of a healer. And so shall the rightful king be known."*

"'Hark!' The herald angels sing: 'Glory to the newborn King!'"

ACKNOWLEDGMENTS

I am indebted to so many people that I do not believe I can adequately thank them all. But I must thank a few.

First and foremost, I would like to thank those who support my work with the Center For Cultural Leadership, without whose generosity the contents of this book would never have been written.

P. Andrew Sandlin not only has graciously welcomed me to work with CCL, but has been a constant friend full of encouragement. Together with Andrew, David Bahnsen and Jeffrey Ventrella have rounded out my cadre of counselors, and a man could ask for no better friends.

My family has endured years of a lack of worldly security, and I am forever amazed and thankful at how comfortable, joyous, and pleasant they make a life of unknowns that should, humanly speaking, produce anxiety. They make me a man of immense wealth. I thank them, and I thank God for them.

ABOUT THE AUTHOR

Brian G. Mattson is a theologian, writer, speaker, guitarist, song-writer, and performer who avidly follows current events, cultural and political, as well as the Minnesota Twins Baseball Club.

He achieved a B.A. from Montana State University-Billings, an M.A.R. from Westminster Theological Seminary, and a Ph.D. in Systematic Theology from King's College, University of Aberdeen.

He lives with his family in Billings, Montana.

www.drbrianmattson.com

Made in United States
Orlando, FL
03 April 2022

16447272R00134